WISDOM OF THE EAST

ANCIENT
EGYPTIAN LEGENDS

BY M. A. MURRAY

ISBN: 978-1-63923-691-6

Printed: February 2023

Published and Distributed By:
Lushena Books
607 Country Club Drive, Unit E
Bensenville, IL 60106
www.lushenabks.com

ISBN: 978-1-63923-691-6

TO

MY STUDENTS, PAST AND PRESENT,

I DEDICATE THIS BOOK

PREFACE

In this book I have retold the legends of the Gods of ancient Egypt, legends, which were current in the "morning of the world," preserved to the present day engraved on stone and written on papyri. I have told them in my own way, adhering strictly to the story, but arranging the words and phrases according to the English method; retaining, however, as far as possible the expressions and metaphors of the Egyptian. In some cases I have inserted whole sentences in order to make the sense clear; these are in places where the story divides naturally into several parts, as in "The Battles of Horus," and "The Regions of Night and Thick Darkness"; where each incident, so like the one preceding and the one following, is kept distinct in the mind of the reader by this means. This repetition is quite in accordance with the style of Egyptian literature.

The book is intended entirely for the general public, who are increasingly interested in the religion and civilisation of ancient Egypt, but whose only means of obtaining knowledge of that country is apparently through magazine stories in which a mummy is the principal character. It may be worth noting that in these legends of ancient Egypt mummies are not mentioned, except in the Duat, the home of the dead, where one naturally expects to find them.

Though the book is intended for the unscientific reader, I have made some provision for the more serious student, in the Notes at the end. In these I have given the origin of the legend, the book or books in which that original is published, and the book where the translation into a modern language by one of the great scholars of the day can be found. Other translations there are in plenty, which can be seen in specialist libraries ; many of these, however, are of use only to a student of Egyptian literature and language.

I have arranged the sequence of the stories according to my own ideas : first, the legends of various, one might almost say miscellaneous, gods ; then the legends of Osiris and the deities connected with him ; lastly, the legends of Ra. At the very end are Notes on the legends, and a short index of all the gods mentioned.

M. A. M.

November 1912

CONTENTS

EDITORIAL NOTE

THE object of the Editors of this series is a very definite one. They desire above all things that, in their humble way, these books shall be the ambassadors of good-will and understanding between East and West—the old world of Thought and the new of Action. In this endeavour, and in their own sphere, they are but followers of the highest example in the land. They are confident that a deeper knowledge of the great ideals and lofty philosophy of Oriental thought may help to a revival of that true spirit of Charity which neither despises nor fears the nation of another creed and colour.

L. CRANMER-BYNG.
S. A. KAPADIA.

NORTHBROOK SOCIETY,
21 CROMWELL ROAD,
KENSINGTON, S.W.

ANCIENT EGYPTIAN LEGENDS

I

THE PRINCESS AND THE DEMON

IT was in the reign of King Rameses, son of the Sun, beloved of Amon, king of the gods. A mighty warrior was Rameses ; in the day of battle like to Mentu, god of war ; very valorous was he, like the son of the Sky-goddess.

Now his Majesty was in Naharaina, where the great river Euphrates rolls down to the sea. And he received the tribute of the vassal-princes, for he was the conqueror of the nine Archer-tribes, and none could stand before his face when he came forth equipped with all his weapons of war. The princes prostrated themselves before him, bowing their foreheads to the ground, breathing the earth which his feet had trodden. Great and splendid was their tribute : gold, and precious stones of all colours, blue lapis lazuli and the green turquoise sacred to Hathor, goddess of love and joy. And slaves came bearing on

11

their backs sweet-scented woods, perfumed and aromatic, like the trees in the land of the Gods.

The prince of Bekhten came also, and with him his eldest daughter ; and he placed her in front of the slaves, for she was the choicest part of his tribute. Very beautiful was she, fair in her limbs, tall and slender as a palm-tree, and the heart of the King turned to her with delight, and he loved her more than anything on earth. He made her the Great Royal Wife, and he gave her a name by which she should be known in the land of Egypt ; Neferu-Ra, " Beauty of Ra," was she called, for her beauty was like the shining of the sun. And the name was written in the royal oval, as is the custom of the kings of Egypt and their queens.

Then King Rameses returned to Egypt, and with him went the Great Royal Wife, Queen Neferu-Ra. And when they came to the Black Land, the land of Egypt, she performed all the ceremonies of a queen in the temples of Egypt.

Now it happened that King Rameses was in Thebes the Mighty on the twenty-second of the month Payni. And he went into the temple of Amon, for this was the day of the beautiful festival of the god, when the boats go up and down upon the water with torches and lights, and the Sacred Barque, adorned with gold and painted with glorious colours, is borne aloft, that men may sce the figure of Amon-Ra himself within. And Queen Neferu-Ra was with his Majesty, for the Great Royal Wife in Egypt has ever been the worshipper of Amon-Ra, king of the gods.

There came into the temple courtiers of the King to announce the arrival of a messenger from the prince of Bekhten. Loaded was he with gifts for Neferu-Ra, Queen of Egypt, daughter of the prince of Bekhten, and he carried also a message to the King. When he entered the royal presence, he bowed to the earth saying, " Glory to thee, O Sun of the nine Archer-tribes! May we live before thee!" Then he bowed to the earth again and spoke the message that he had brought from the prince of Bekhten to Rameses, King of Egypt :

"I come to thee, O living King, my Lord, on account of Bent-reshy, the little sister of the Great Royal Wife, Neferu-Ra ; for there is a malady in all her limbs. Send therefore a learned man that he may see and heal her."

The King turned to his courtiers and said, " Bring hither a scribe of the House of Life, and bring also those who speak the hidden things of the Inner Chamber." And the courtiers hastened and brought them into the presence forthwith, and the King said to them, " I have brought you hither to hear this matter. Tell me then of a man, learned and skilful, to send to the prince of Bekhten."

Then they took counsel among themselves as

to a learned and skilful man, and they brought the scribe Tehuti-em-heb before the King, and the King bade him go with the messenger of the prince of Bekhten to heal Bent-reshy, the little sister of the Great Royal Wife.

When the scribe Tehuti-em-heb came to Bekhten, he was brought into the presence of Bent-reshy. He was a learned and a skilful man, and he found the princess under the dominion of a spirit, a spirit that was hostile to him, against whom his learning and skill were of no avail, who set his magic arts at naught.

Then the prince of Bekhten was sad, and sorrow was in his heart, but Tehuti-em-heb the scribe counselled him to send again to Egypt and to implore the help of Khonsu, the Expeller of Demons, to cast out the evil spirit from Bent-reshy, the little sister of the Great Royal Wife.

Now so great was the distance from Bekhten to Egypt that from the time that Tehuti-em-heb the scribe departed out of Thebes till the second message came to King Rameses was three years, and throughout that time the evil spirit dwelt in Bent-reshy and would not be cast out.

And when the second messenger arrived, King Rameses was again in Thebes, and it was the first of the month Pakhons, the month that is sacred to Khonsu. He entered into the temple, and with him came his courtiers, and the messenger of the prince of Bekhten. In the temple were two statues of Khonsu; very marvellous figures were these, very sacred, very holy; the one was called Khonsu in Thebes Neferhotep, and the other Khonsu, the Expeller of Demons. Now Khonsu is the God of the Moon, the son of Amon-Ra and of Mut, Lady of Ashru, and men represent him with the curled lock of youth, for he is ever young and beautiful.

Then the King stood before the great statue of Khonsu in Thebes Neferhotep and said, " O my good Lord, I come again into thy presence on account of the daughter of the prince of Bekhten."

Then the priests lifted the statue of Khonsu in Thebes Neferhotep and placed it in front of Khonsu, the Expeller of Demons. And the King spoke again before Khonsu in Thebes Neferhotep and said, "My good Lord, turn thy face to Khonsu, the Expeller of Demons. Grant that he may go to Bekhten."

Khonsu in Thebes Neferhotep inclined his head twice in token of assent. Very marvellous was the figure of Khonsu in Thebes Neferhotep.

And yet again King Rameses spoke, " Let thy protection be with him. Grant that I may send the Majesty of Khonsu to Bekhten to save Bent-reshy, the little sister of the Great Royal Wife."

Khonsu in Thebes Neferhotep inclined his head twice in token of assent. Very marvellous

was the figure of Khonsu in Thebes Neferhotep.
And he gave his magical protection four times
to Khonsu, the Expeller of Demons.

Then King Rameses gave command, and
Khonsu, the Expeller of Demons, was placed in
the Great Boat ; and around the Great Boat were
five small boats, with chariots and horses, numerous and splendid, on the right hand and on the
left. The retinue of Khonsu, the Expeller of
Demons, was the retinue of a king. For a year and
five months they journeyed until they reached
Bekhten.

The prince of Bekhten came out with his bow-
men and his courtiers to meet Khonsu, the Expeller of Demons, with a royal welcome, and they
entered into his presence as into the presence of
a king. The prince of Bekhten fell on his knees
and laid his forehead on the ground at the feet
of Khonsu, the Expeller of Demons, and said,
"Thou hast come to us. O, be kind to us according to the words of Rameses, King of Egypt."

They brought Khonsu, the Expeller of Demons,
to the chamber of Bent-reshy, the little sister of
the Great Royal Wife ; and he made a magical
protection over her. Lo, there happened a wonder
and a marvel, for she was well and whole in a
moment.

Then the spirit, who had been in her, spoke in
the presence of Khonsu, the Expeller of Demons,
"Thou hast come in peace, O great God, Expeller

of Demons. Bekhten is thy city, its people are thy slaves. I bow before thee, for I also am thy slave. I will go to that place from which I came that thy heart may have peace. But ere I go, let the Majesty of Khonsu give command that a holy day be made for me by the prince of Bekhten."

When he had heard these words, Khonsu, the Expeller of Demons, inclined his head to the priest and said, " Let the prince of Bekhten make a great sacrifice for this spirit."

The prince of Bekhten, and his soldiers and his courtiers heard the voices of the spirit and of the god, and they trembled and were exceedingly afraid. They obeyed the command of the god and prepared a great sacrifice for Khonsu, the Expeller of Demons, and for the spirit that came out of Bent-reshy, the little sister of the Great Royal Wife, the daughter of the prince of Bekhten. And they made a holy day with offerings, sacrifices, and libations.

So the spirit, in the form of a Shining One, went his way in peace out of the land of Bekhten, and he went whithersoever it pleased him, as Khonsu, the Expeller of Demons, had commanded.

The prince of Bekhten was glad and his heart rejoiced, and all the people rejoiced also that the spirit had been driven out of Bent-reshy and out of the land of Bekhten. But in the midst of

2

his joy and gladness, fear came upon the heart of the prince of Bekhten lest the spirit should return and take up his abode again in the land, when Khonsu, the Expeller of Demons, had departed. He took counsel with himself and said, " I will keep Khonsu, the Expeller of Demons, in Bekhten. I will not let him return to Egypt." So Khonsu, the Expeller of Demons, remained three years, four months, and five days in Bekhten, for the prince of Bekhten would not let him go.

And at the end of that time the prince of Bekhten lay upon his bed at night and slept, and while he slept a vision passed before his eyes. He dreamed that he stood before the shrine of Khonsu, the Expeller of Demons ; the great doors of the shrine were folded back and the god came forth, stepping out between the doors. He changed into the form of a hawk with feathers of gold, burnished and beautiful, and soared high into the air with wings outspread, and like an arrow he darted towards Egypt.

When the prince of Bekhten awoke, he was exceedingly afraid, for he feared the wrath of the Gods. And he sent for the priest of Khonsu, the Expeller of Demons, and said to him, " The god is estranged from us, he has returned to Egypt. Let his chariot also return to Egypt." The prince of Bekhten gave command that the god should be taken back to Egypt, and he loaded the god with gifts. Great and numerous were the gifts of all manner of beautiful things that the prince of Bekhten gave to Khonsu, the Expeller of Demons.

For many months they journeyed, and with them went an escort of soldiers and horses from the land of Bekhten. They arrived in safety at Thebes, and entered into the temple of Khonsu in Thebes Neferhotep.

Then Khonsu, the Expeller of Demons, gave to Khonsu in Thebes Neferhotep all the gifts, the rich and costly gifts, which he had received from the prince of Bekhten; nothing did he keep for himself. Thus ended the journey of Khonsu, the Expeller of Demons, the great God.

II

THE KING'S DREAM

Long, long ago lived Thothmes, King of Egypt; Lord of the Two Lands was he, Wearer of the double Diadem, he whom the Gods loved. He was not that Thothmes, the mighty Bull, who conquered Syria, Nubia, and the nine Archer-tribes. But he bore the same name, and was a great and valorous king; Syria bowed before him, Nubia was his servant, and he trod the nine Archer-tribes beneath his feet. When he was a child, he was like unto Harpocrates, the son of Isis, he who was born in the marshes of the North Country. Beautiful was he with the beauty of the Gods, in form like Horus, the Avenger of his father.

And in all manly sports did he excel; he hunted the wild game on the deserts both north and south of Memphis, he coursed the lions and the deer, he shot arrows at a target, he drove in his chariot, and his horses were fleeter than the wind. Alone did he hunt, or with two companions only, and none knew the path that he

would follow, for in the desert none live save
wild beasts.

When his followers required rest in the heat of
the day, he took them to the great statue of
Harmachis close to Kher-aha, where the Road of
the God leads eastward to On. Of stone was
this mighty figure, hewn out of the living rock,
his face the face of a man, stern and majestic,
turned to the rising sun, his body the body of a
lion ; upon his brow is the death-dealing snake
with head erect, ready to strike. Men call this
figure Harmachis, and the Sphinx, and the
Father of Terrors. Great and exalted is this
figure of the God, resting in his chosen place ;
mighty is his power, for the Shadow of the Sun
is upon him. The temples of Memphis and the
temples of every town on both sides adore him,
they stretch out their hands to him in adoration,
sacrifices and libations are made before him.

One day, ere Thothmes was yet king, before
he had ascended the throne of Horus the Living
One, it came to pass that he hunted alone in the
desert, and it was noontide. Very fierce was the
heat, very blinding the sunbeams, and he rested
in the shadow of the great God. And as he rested,
heated and weary, in the coolness of the shadow,
sleep heavy and deep came upon him at the
moment when the sun reached the zenith.

Thus he slept at broad midday, and in his sleep
dreams and visions came to him. In his dream

he stood before the giant figure of the God, but no longer was it of stone, for behold it was the God himself. The breath of life was in him, and his lips moved, and he spoke with gentle speech as a father speaks with his child, for his words were words of blessing.

"See now, O my son Thothmes," he said, "look at me, behold me. I am thy father, I who am Harmachis, and Ra, and Khepera, and Atmu also. For I am the Sun-god to whom all lands are subject. Through me alone shall the kingdom of Egypt come to thee ; thou shalt wear the White Crown of the South Land and the Red Crown of the North Land, thou shalt sit upon the throne of Geb the inheritor. To thee shall belong the whole land in its length and breadth, that land which the universal Lord makes glorious. Want and trouble shall never come nigh thee, for gifts shall be brought to thee from every country, near and afar ; the duration of thy life shall be for many years ; my face shall be towards thee and my heart shall incline to thee if thou wilt do for me that which I desire of thee."

And Thothmes looked, and he saw that the figure lay half-buried in the sand, and it seemed as though the God struggled to free himself, for naught but the head appeared above the plain, and the sands came up about him like the waves of the sea when they swallow up a ship that is on the rocks.

Then the Majesty of the God spoke again, and said, "The sand of the desert on which I rest is about me, it overwhelms me, it covers me. Hasten to do that which my heart desires, for I know that thou art a son who honours the behests of his father."

Sleep fell from the eyelids of Thothmes, and he awoke.

[Here the inscription is broken away and the end of the story is not known.]

III

THE COMING OF THE GREAT QUEEN

Now Amon-Ra, king of the gods, sat upon his throne, and around him stood the greatest of the gods and goddesses. On his right was Osiris crowned with the great White Crown of the South Land ; on his left was Mentu, god of war, and on the head of Mentu were two great feathers and the flashing disk of the sun. With Osiris were the twin goddesses Isis and Nephthys, beside them stood Hathor, goddess of love, whom the Greeks call Aphrodite ; Horus, the son of Isis, with the far-seeing eyes of the hawk ; and Anubis, son of Nephthys, the faithful guardian of Isis. With Mentu were Atmu, the god of the sunset ; Shu and his twin-sister Tefnut ; Geb the earth-god, and Nut the sky-goddess. These two are the oldest of the gods, from whom all others proceed.

Amon-Ra, king of the gods, sat upon his throne and looked upon the land of Egypt, and he spoke, saying, " I will create a queen to rule over Tamery, I will unite the Two Lands in peace for her, and in her hands I will place the whole world. Egypt and Syria, Nubia and Punt, the land of the Gods, shall be under her sway." And when he had spoken there was silence among the gods.

While he yet spoke, Thoth entered into his presence, Thoth, the twice-great, the maker of magic, the lord of Khemennu. He listened to the words of Amon-Ra, king of the gods, and in the silence that followed he spoke:

" O Amon-Ra, Lord of the thrones of the Two Lands, King of the gods, Maker of men. Behold in the Black Land in the palace of the king is a maiden, fair and beautiful is she in all her limbs. Aahmes is her name, and she is wife to the king of Egypt. She alone can be the mother of the great Queen, whom thou wilt create to rule over the Two Lands. She is in the palace of the king. Come, let us go to her."

Now the form of Thoth is the form of an ibis, that he may fly swiftly through the air and none may know him, and as an ibis he went to the palace of the king. But Amon-Ra took upon himself the shape of the king of Egypt. Great was the majesty of Amon-Ra, splendid his adornments. On his neck was the glittering collar of gold and precious stones, on his arms were bracelets of pure gold and electrum, and on his head were two plumes ; by the plumes alone could men know the King of the gods. In one hand he carried the sceptre of power, in the other the emblem of life. Glorious was he as the sun at midday, and the perfumes of the land of Punt were around him.

In the palace of the king of Egypt was queen Aahmes, and it was night. She lay upon her couch, and sleep was upon her eyelids. Like a jewel was she in her beauty, and the chamber in which she slept was like the setting of the jewel ; black bronze and electrum, acacia wood and ebony, were the adornments of the palace, and her couch was in the form of a fierce lion.

Through the two Great Doors of the palace went the gods ; none saw them, none beheld them. And with them came Neith, goddess of Sais, and Selk the scorpion goddess. On the head of Neith were the shield and crossed arrows ; on the head of Selk a scorpion bearing in each claw the emblem of life.

The fragrance of the perfumes of Punt filled the chamber, and queen Aahmes awoke and beheld Amon-Ra, King of the gods, Maker of men. In majesty and beauty he appeared before her, and her heart was filled with joy. He held towards her the sign of life, and in her hand he laid the sign of life and the sceptre of power. And Neith and Selk lifted the couch on which the queen reposed and held it high in the air, that she might be raised above the ground, on which mortal men live, while she spoke with the immortal Gods.

Then Amon-Ra returned and was enthroned among the Gods. And he summoned to his presence Khnum the creator, he who fashions the bodies of men, who dwells beside the rushing waters of the cataract. To Khnum he gave command saying, " O Khnum, fashioner of the bodies of men, fashion for me my daughter, she who shall be the great Queen of Egypt. For I will give to her all life and satisfaction, all stability and all joy of heart for ever."

Khnum the creator, the fashioner of the bodies of men, the dweller by the cataract, made answer to Amon-Ra, " I will form for thee thy daughter, and her form shall be more glorious than the Gods, for the greatness of her dignity as King of the South and North."

Then he brought his potter's wheel, and took clay, and with his hands he fashioned the body of the daughter of queen Aahmes and the body of her *ka*. And the body of the child and the body of the *ka* were alike in their limbs and their faces, and none but the Gods could know them apart. Beautiful were they with the beauty of Amon-Ra, more glorious were they than the Gods.

Beside the potter's wheel knelt Hekt, lady of Herur, goddess of birth. In each hand she held the sign of life, and as the wheel turned and the bodies were fashioned, she held it towards them that life might enter into the lifeless clay.

Then Khnum, the fashioner of the bodies of

men, and Hekt the goddess of birth, came to
the palace of the king of Egypt ; and with them
came Isis, the great Mother, and her sister
Nephthys ; Meskhent also and Ta-urt, and Bes
the protector of children.   The spirits of Pé and
the spirits of Dep came with them to greet the
daughter of Amon-Ra and of queen Aahmes.

And when the child appeared, the goddesses rejoiced, and the spirits of Pé and the spirits of Dep
chanted praises to her honour, for the daughter
of Amon-Ra was to sit upon the throne of Horus
of the Living, and rule the Land of Egypt to the
glory of the Gods.   Hatshepsut was she called,
Chief of Noble Women, divine of Diadems,
favourite of the Goddesses, beloved of Amon-Ra.
And to her the Gods granted that she should be
mistress of all lands within the circuit of the sun,
and that she should appear as king upon the throne
of Horus before the glories of the Great House.
And upon her was the favour of Amon-Ra for
ever.

IV

THE BOOK OF THOTH

Now Ahura was the wife of Nefer-ka-ptah, and their child was Merab; this was the name by which he was registered by the scribes in the House of Life. And Nefer-ka-ptah, though he was the son of the King, cared for naught on earth but to read the ancient records, written on papyrus in the House of Life or engraved on stone in the temples; all day and every day he studied the writings of the ancestors.

One day he went into the temple to pray to the Gods, but when he saw the inscriptions on the walls he began to read them; and he forgot to pray, he forgot the Gods, he forgot the priests, he forgot all that was around him until he heard laughter behind him. He looked round and a priest stood there, and from him came the laughter.

"Why laughest thou at me?" said Nefer-ka-ptah.

"Because thou readest these worthless writings," answered the priest. "If thou wouldest read writings that are worth the reading I can tell thee where the Book of Thoth lies hidden."

Then Nefer-ka-ptah was eager in his questions, and the priest replied, "Thoth wrote the Book with his own hand, and in it is all the magic in the world. If thou readest the first page, thou wilt enchant the sky, the earth, the abyss, the mountains, and the sea ; thou wilt understand the language of the birds of the air, and thou wilt know what the creeping things of earth are saying, and thou wilt see the fishes from the darkest depths of the sea. And if thou readest the other page, even though thou wert dead and in the world of ghosts, thou couldest come back to earth in the form thou once hadst. And besides this, thou wilt see the sun shining in the sky with the full moon and the stars, and thou wilt behold the great shapes of the Gods."

Then said Nefer-ka-ptah, "By the life of Pharaoh, that Book shall be mine. Tell me whatsoever it is that thou desirest, and I will do it for thee."

"Provide for my funeral," said the priest. "See that I am buried as a rich man, with priests and mourning women, offerings, libations, and incense. Then shall my soul rest in peace in the Fields of Aalu. One hundred pieces of silver must be spent upon my burying."

Then Nefer-ka-ptah sent a fleet messenger to fetch the money, and he paid one hundred pieces

of silver into the priest's hands.   When the priest
had taken the silver, he said to Nefer-ka-ptah :
"The Book is at Koptos in the middle of the river.
In the middle of the river is an iron box,
In the iron box is a bronze box,
In the bronze box is a keté-wood box,
In the keté-wood box is an ivory-and-ebony box,
In the ivory-and-ebony box is a silver box,
In the silver box is a gold box,
And in the gold box is the Book of Thoth.
Round about the great iron box are snakes and
scorpions and all manner of crawling things, and
above all there is a snake which no man can kill.
These are set to guard the Book of Thoth."

When the priest had finished speaking, Nefer-
ka-ptah ran out of the temple, for his joy was
so great that he knew not where he was.   He
ran quickly to find Ahura to tell her about
the Book and that he would go to Koptos and
find it.

But Ahura was very sorrowful, and said, "Go
not on this journey, for trouble and grief await
thee in the Southern Land."

She laid her hand upon Nefer-ka-ptah as though
she would hold him back from the sorrow that
awaited him.   But he would not be restrained,
and broke away from her and went to the King
his father.

He told the King all that he had learned, and
said, "Give me the royal barge, O my father,

that I may go to the Southern Land with my wife Ahura and my son Merab. For the Book of Thoth I must and will have."

So the King gave orders and the royal barge was prepared, and in it Nefer-ka-ptah, Ahura, and Merab sailed up the river to the Southern Land as far as Koptos. When they arrived at Koptos, the high priest and all the priests of Isis of Koptos came down to the river to welcome Nefer-ka-ptah, Ahura, and Merab. And they went in a great procession to the temple of the Goddess, and Nefer-ka-ptah sacrificed an ox and a goose and poured a libation of wine to Isis of Koptos and her son Harpocrates. After this, the priests of Isis and their wives made a great feast for four days in honour of Nefer-ka-ptah and Ahura.

On the morning of the fifth day, Nefer-ka-ptah called to him a priest of Isis, a great magician learned in all the mysteries of the Gods. And together they made a little magic box, like the cabin of a boat, and they made men and a great store of tackle, and put the men and the tackle in the magic cabin. Then they uttered a spell over the cabin, and the men breathed and were alive, and began to use the tackle. And Nefer-ka-ptah sank the magic cabin in the river, saying, "Workmen, workmen! Work for me!" And he filled the royal barge with sand and sailed away alone, while Ahura sat on the bank of the river at Koptos, and watched and waited, for she knew that sorrow must come of this journey to the Southern Land.

The magic men in the magic cabin toiled all night and all day for three nights and three days along the bottom of the river; and when they stopped the royal barge stopped also, and Nefer-ka-ptah knew that he had arrived where the Book lay hidden.

He took the sand out of the royal barge and threw it into the water, and it made a gap in the river, a gap of a schoenus long and a schoenus wide; in the middle of the gap lay the iron box, and beside the box was coiled the great snake that no man can kill, and all around the box on every side to the edge of the walls of water were snakes and scorpions and all manner of crawling things.

Then Nefer-ka-ptah stood up in the royal barge, and across the water he cried to the snakes and scorpions and crawling things; a loud and terrib'e cry, and the words were words of magic. As soon as his voice was still, the snakes and scorpions and crawling things were still also, for they were enchanted by means of the magical words of Nefer-ka-ptah, and they could not move. Nefer-ka-ptah brought the royal barge to the edge of the gap, and he walked through the snakes and scorpions and crawling things, and they looked at him, but could not move because of the spell that was on them.

And now Nefer-ka-ptah was face to face with

3

the snake that no man could kill, and it reared
itself up ready for battle. Nefer-ka-ptah rushed
upon it and cut off its head, and at once the head
and body came together, each to each, and the
snake that no man could kill was alive again, and
ready for the fray. Again Nefer-ka-ptah rushed
upon it, and so hard did he strike that the head
was flung far from the body, but at once the head
and body came together again, each to each, and
again the snake that no man could kill was alive
and ready to fight. Then Nefer-ka-ptah saw that
the snake was immortal and could not be slain,
but must be overcome by subtle means. Again
he rushed upon it and cut it in two, and very
quickly he put sand on each part, so that when
the head and body came together there was
sand between them and they could not join, and
the snake that no man could kill lay helpless
before him.

Then Nefer-ka-ptah went to the great box where
it stood in the gap in the middle of the river,
and the snakes and scorpions and crawling things
watched, but they could not stop him.

He opened the iron box and found a bronze box,

He opened the bronze box and found a keté-wood
box,

He opened the keté-wood box and found an
ivory-and-ebony box,

He opened the ivory-and-ebony box and found
a silver box,

He opened the silver box and found a gold box,

He opened the gold box and found the Book of Thoth.

He opened the Book and read a page, and at once he had enchanted the sky, the earth, the abyss, the mountains, and the sea, and he understood the language of birds, fish, and beasts. He read the second page and he saw the sun shining in the sky, with the full moon and the stars, and he saw the great shapes of the Gods themselves ; and so strong was the magic that the fishes came up from the darkest depths of the sea. So he knew that what the priest had told him was true.

Then he thought of Ahura waiting for him at Koptos, and he cast a magic spell upon the men that he had made, saying " Workmen, workmen ! Work for me ! and take me back to the place from which I came." They toiled day and night till they came to Koptos, and there was Ahura sitting by the river, having eaten nothing and drunk nothing since Nefer-ka-ptah went away. For she sat waiting and watching for the sorrow that was to come upon them.

But when she saw Nefer-ka-ptah returning in the royal barge, her heart was glad and she rejoiced exceedingly. Nefer-ka-ptah came to her and put the Book of Thoth into her hands and bade her read it. When she read the first page, she enchanted the sky, the earth, the abyss, the mountains, and the sea, and she understood the language of birds, fish, and beasts ; and when she read the second page, she saw the sun shining in the sky, with the full moon and the stars, and she saw the great shapes of the Gods themselves ; and so strong was the magic that the fishes came up from the darkest depths of the sea.

Nefer-ka-ptah now called for a piece of new papyrus and for a cup of beer ; and on the papyrus he wrote all the spells that were in the Book of Thoth.   Then he took the cup of beer and washed the papyrus in the beer, so that all the ink was washed off and the papyrus became as though it had never been written on.   And Nefer-ka-ptah drank the beer, and at once he knew all the spells that had been written on the papyrus, for this is the method of the great magicians.

Then Nefer-ka-ptah and Ahura went to the temple of Isis and gave offerings to Isis and Harpocrates, and made a great feast, and the next day they went on board the royal barge and sailed joyfully away down the river towards the Northern Land.

But behold, Thoth had discovered the loss of his Book, and Thoth raged like a panther of the South, and he hastened before Ra and told him all, saying, " Nefer-ka-ptah has found my magic box and opened it, and has stolen my Book, even the Book of Thoth ; he slew the guards that surrounded it, and the snake that no man can kill lay helpless before him. Avenge me, O Ra, upon Nefer-ka-ptah, son of the King of Egypt."

The Majesty of Ra answered and said, " Take him and his wife and his child, and do with them as thou wilt." And now the sorrow for which Ahura watched and waited was about to come upon them, for Thoth took with him a Power from Ra to give him his desire upon the stealer of his Book.

As the royal barge sailed smoothly down the river, the little boy Merab ran out from the shade of the awning and leaned over the side watching the water. And the Power of Ra drew him, so that he fell into the river and was drowned. When he fell, all the sailors on the royal barge and all the people walking on the river-bank raised a great cry, but they could not save him. Nefer-ka-ptah came out of the cabin and read a magical spell over the water, and the body of Merab came to the surface and they brought it on board the royal barge. Then Nefer-ka-ptah read another spell, and so great was its power that the dead child spoke and told Nefer-ka-ptah all that had happened among the Gods, that Thoth was seeking vengeance, and that Ra had granted him his desire upon the stealer of his Book.

Nefer-ka-ptah gave command, and the royal barge returned to Koptos, that Merab might be buried there with the honour due to the son of a prince. When the funeral ceremonies were over, the royal barge sailed down the river towards the Northern Land. A joyful journey was it no longer, for Merab was dead, and Ahura's heart was heavy on account of the sorrow that was still to come, for the vengeance of Thoth was not yet fulfilled.

They reached the place where Merab had fallen into the water, and Ahura came out from under the shade of the awning, and she leaned over the side of the barge, and the Power of Ra drew her so that she fell into the river and was drowned. When she fell, all the sailors in the royal barge and all the people walking on the river-bank raised a great cry, but they could not save her. Nefer-ka-ptah came out of the cabin and read a magical spell over the water, and the body of Ahura came to the surface, and they brought it on board the royal barge. Then Nefer-ka-ptah read another spell, and so great was its power that the dead woman spoke and told Nefer-ka-ptah all that had happened among the Gods, that Thoth was still seeking vengeance, and that Ra had granted him his desire upon the stealer of his Book.

Nefer-ka-ptah gave command and the royal barge returned to Koptos, that Ahura might be buried there with the honour due to the daughter of a king. When the funeral ceremonies were over, the royal barge sailed down the river towards the Northern Land. A sorrowful journey was it

now, for Ahura and Merab were dead, and the
vengeance of Thoth was not yet fulfilled.

They reached the place where Ahura and Merab
had fallen into the water, and Nefer-ka-ptah felt
the Power of Ra drawing him. Though he
struggled against it he knew that it would conquer
him. He took a piece of royal linen, fine and
strong, and made it into a girdle, and with it he
bound the Book of Thoth firmly to his breast,
for he was resolved that Thoth should never
have his Book again.

Then the Power drew him yet more strongly,
and he came from under the shade of the awning
and threw himself into the river and was drowned.
When he fell, all the sailors of the royal barge
and all the people walking on the river-bank raised
a great cry, but they could not save him. And
when they looked for his body they could not find
it. So the royal barge sailed down the river till
they reached the Northern Land and came to
Memphis, and the chiefs of the royal barge went
to the King and told him all that had happened.

The King put on mourning raiment ; he and
his courtiers, the high priest and all the priests
of Memphis, the King's army and the King's
household, were clothed in mourning apparel,
and they walked in procession to the haven of
Memphis to the royal barge. When they came
to the haven, they saw the body of Nefer-ka-ptah
floating in the water beside the barge, close to

the great steering-oars. And this marvel came
to pass because of the magical powers of Nefer-
ka-ptah ; even in death he was a great magician
by reason of the spells he had washed off the
papyrus and drunk in the beer.

Then they drew him out of the water, and they
saw the Book of Thoth bound to his breast with
the girdle of royal linen. And the King gave
command that they should bury Nefer-ka-ptah
with the honour due to the son of a king, and that
the Book of Thoth should be buried with him.

Thus was the vengeance of Thoth fulfilled, but
the Book remained with Nefer-ka-ptah.

V

OSIRIS

IN the beginning Ra cursed Nut, and his curse was that none of her children should be born on any day of any year. And Nut cried to Thoth who loved her, Thoth, the twice great, god of magic and learning and wisdom, he whom the Greeks called Hermes Trismegistos. Though the curse of the great God Ra once uttered could never be recalled, Thoth by his wisdom opened a way of escape. He went to the Moon-god, whose brightness was almost equal to that of the Sun itself, and challenged him to a game of dice. Great were the stakes on either side, but the Moon's were the greatest, for he wagered his own light. Game after game they played and always the luck was with Thoth, till the Moon would play no more. Then Thoth, the twice great, gathered up the light he had won, and by his power and might he formed it into five days. And since that time the Moon has not had light enough to shine throughout the month; but dwindles away into darkness, and then comes slowly to his full glory ; for the light of five whole days was taken from him. And these five days Thoth placed between the end of the old year and the beginning of the new year, keeping them distinct from both ; and on these five days the five children of Nut were born ; Osiris on the first day, Horus on the second, Set on the third, Isis on the fourth, and Nephthys on the fifth. Thus the curse of Ra was both fulfilled and made of no effect, for the days on which the children of Nut were born belonged to no year.

When Osiris was born, wonders and marvels, prodigies and signs, were heard and seen throughout the world, for a voice cried over the whol earth, " The Lord of all comes forth to the light.' And a woman drawing water from the hol place of the temple was filled with the divin afflatus and rushed forth crying, " Osiris the Kin is born."

Now Egypt was a barbarous country wher men fought together and ate human flesh ; naugh did they know of the gods, lawless were the and savage. But Osiris became the King o Egypt, and he showed his people how to till th land and to plant corn and the vine, and h taught them the honour due to the Gods, an made laws, and abolished their barbarous an savage customs. Wherever he went, the peopl bowed at his feet, for they loved the very groun he trod on ; and whatever he commanded, tha they did. Thus did Osiris rule over the Egyptians till, with music playing and banners flying, he passed out of Egypt to bring all nations beneath his gracious sway.

But Set hated his brother Osiris, and he gathered to himself seventy-two conspirators, and with them was Aso, queen of Ethiopia. And they made a plan that when Osiris returned they should kill him and place Set on the throne; but they hid their plans, and with smiling faces went out to meet Osiris when he re-entered Egypt in triumph.

In secret they met again and again, in secret also they prepared a coffer made of costly wood painted and decorated with rich designs and glowing colours, an interweaving of tints and a wealth of cunning workmanship, so that all who saw it longed to have it for their own. Set, that Wicked One, had in secret measured the body of Osiris, and the coffer was made to fit the body of the King, for this was part of the plan.

When all was ready, Set bade his brother and the seventy-two conspirators to a feast in his great banqueting-hall. When the feast was over, they sang the chant of Maneros, as was the custom, and slaves carried round cups of wine and threw garlands of flowers round the necks of the guests, and poured perfume upon them, till the hall was filled with sweet odours. And while their hearts were glad, slaves entered bearing the coffer, and all the guests cried out at the sight of its beauty.

Then Set stood up in his place and said, " He who lies down in this coffer and whom it fits, to that man I will give it." His words were sweet as honey, but in his heart was the bitterness of evil.

One after one, the conspirators lay down in the coffer with jests and laughter ; for one it was too long, and for another it was too short, and for a third it was too wide, and for a fourth too narrow. Then came Osiris to take his turn, and he, all unsuspecting, lay down in it. At once the conspirators seized the lid and clapped it on ; some nailed it firmly in its place, while others poured molten lead into all the openings lest he should breathe and live. Thus died the great Osiris, he who is called Unnefer the Triumphant, and by his death he entered into the Duat, and became King of the Dead and Ruler of those who are in the West.

The conspirators lifted the chest, which was now a coffin, and carried it to the river-bank. They flung it far into the water, and Hapi the Nile-god caught it and carried it upon his stream to the sea ; the Great Green Waters received it and the waves bore it to Byblos and lifted it into a tamarisk-tree that grew by the shore. Then the tree shot forth great branches and put out leaves and flowers to make a fit resting-place for the God, and the fame of its beauty went throughout the land.

In Byblos ruled King Malkander and his wife, Queen Athenais. They came to the sea-shore to gaze upon the tree, for naught could be seen but leaves and blossoms which hid the coffin from all eyes. Then King Malkander gave command and the tree was cut down and carried to the royal palace to make a pillar therein, for it was worthy to be used in a king's house. All men wondered at its beauty, though none knew that it held the body of a God.

Now Isis feared Set exceedingly. His smooth words did not deceive her, and she knew of his enmity to Osiris, but the great King would not believe in his brother's wickedness. When the soul of Osiris passed from his body, at once Isis was aware that he was dead, though no man told her. She took her little son, whom men call Harpocrates or Horus the Child, and fled with him to the marshes of the Delta, and hid him in the city of Pé. Ancient and gray was this city of Pé and it stood on an island; there dwelt the goddess Uazet, whom men call also Buto and Latona, for she is worshipped under many names. Uazet took the child and sheltered him, and Isis by her divine power loosed the island from its moorings, and it floated on the surface of the Great Green Waters, so that no man could tell where to find it. For she feared the power of

Set lest he should destroy the child as he had destroyed the father.

As the souls of men cannot rest until the funeral rites are performed and the funeral sacrifices offered, she journeyed, solitary and alone, to seek the body of her husband, and bury it as became his greatness. Many people did she meet, both men and women, but none had seen the chest, and in this matter her power was of no avail. Then she thought to ask the children, and at once they told her of a painted coffer floating on the Nile. And to this day children have prophetic power and can declare the will of the Gods and the things that are yet for to come.

Thus, asking always of the children, Isis came to Byblos. She sat by the Great Green Waters, and the maidens of Queen Athenais came to bathe and disport themselves in the waves. Then Isis spoke to them and braided their hair and adjusted their jewels; the breath of the Goddess was sweeter than the odours of the Land of Punt, and it perfumed the hair and the jewels and the garments of the maidens. When they returned to the palace, Queen Athenais asked them whence they had obtained the perfume, and they answered, " A woman, strange and sad, sat by the sea-shore when we went to bathe, and she braided our hair and adjusted our jewels, and from her came the perfume, though we know not how." Queen Athenais went to the shore to see the strange woman and conversed with her, and they spoke together as mothers speak, for each had a little son ; the son of Isis was far away and the son of Athenais was sick unto death.

Then rose up Isis, the Mighty in Magic, the skilful Healer, and said, " Bring me to your son ! " Together the Goddess and the Queen returned to the palace, and Isis took little Diktys in her arms and said, " I can make him strong and well, but in my own way will I do it, and none must interfere."

Every day Queen Athenais marvelled at her son. From a little puling babe he became a strong and healthy child, but Isis spoke no word and none knew what she did. Athenais questioned her maidens, and they answered, " We know not what she does, but this we know, that she feeds him not, and at night she bars the doors of the hall of the pillar, and piles the fire high with logs, and when we listen, naught can we hear but the twittering of a swallow."

Athenais was filled with curiosity and hid herself at night in the great hall, and watched how Isis barred the doors and piled the logs upon the fire till the flames rose high and scorching. Then, sitting before the fire, she made a space between the blazing logs, a space that glowed red and crimson, and in that space she laid the child, and turning herself into the form of a swallow, she circled round the pillar, mourning and lamenting,

and the lamentation was like the twitterin
of a swallow. Queen Athenais shrieked an
snatched the child from the fire, and turned t
flee. But before her stood Isis the Goddess, ta
and terrible.

" O foolish mother ! " said Isis. " Why did
thou seize the child ? But a few days longer an
all that is mortal in him would have been buri
away, and as the Gods would he have bee
immortal and for ever young."

A great awe fell upon the Queen, for she kne
that she looked upon one of the Gods. In hum
blest wise she and King Malkander prayed tl
Goddess to accept a gift. All the riches of Bybl
were spread before her, but to her they were a
naught.

" Give me," she said, " what this pillar hold
and I shall be content." At once the workme
were summoned, and they took down the pilla1
and split it open, and lifted out the coffin. An
Isis took sweet spices and scented blossoms
these she strewed upon the pillar, then wrappe
it in fine linen and gave it to the King and Queer
And all the people of Byblos worship it to this da）
because once it held the body of a god.

But Isis took the coffin on a boat and saile
away from Byblos, and when the waves of th
river Phaedrus, lashed by the wind, threatene
to sweep the coffin away, she dried up the wate
by her magical spells. Then, in a solitary plac（

she opened the coffin, and, gazing upon the face
of the dead God, she mourned and lamented.

Now some say that when Isis left Byblos she
took Diktys with her, and that he fell out of the
boat and was drowned. Others say that the
sound of her lamentation was so terrible in its
grief that his heart broke and he died. But I
think that he remained in Byblos ; and because
he had lain in the arms of the Divine Mother, and
had passed through the purifying fire, he grew
up to be a great and noble King, ruling his people
wisely.

Then Isis hid the coffin and set out for the city
of Pé, where it stood on the floating island and
where her little son Harpocrates was safe under
the care of Uazet, the Goddess of the North Country. And while she was away, Set came hunting
wild boars with his dogs. He hunted by moonlight,
for he loved the night, when all evil red things
are abroad ; and the air was filled with the whoop
and halloa of the huntsman and the cries of the
dogs as they rushed after their quarry. And as
he dashed past, Set saw the painted chest, the
colours glinting and gleaming in the moonlight.

At that sight, hatred and anger came upon him
like a red cloud, and he raged like a panther of
the South. He dragged the coffin from the place
where it was hidden and forced it open ; he
seized the body and tore it into fourteen pieces,
and by his mighty and divine strength he scattered

4

the pieces throughout the land of Egypt. And
he laughed and said, " It is not possible to destroy
the body of a God, but I have done what is im-
possible, I have destroyed Osiris." And his
laughter echoed across the world, and those who
heard it fled trembling.

When Isis returned, she found naught but the
broken coffin, and knew that Set had done this
thing. All her search was now to begin again.
She took a little shallop made of papyrus-reeds
lashed together, and sailed through the marshes
to look for the pieces of Osiris' body, and all the
birds and beasts went with her to help her ; and
to this day the crocodiles will not touch a boat
of papyrus-reeds, for they think it is the weary
Goddess still pursuing her search.

A mighty and a cunning enemy was hers, and
by wisdom only could he be overcome ; therefore,
wheresoever she found a fragment of the divine
body, she built a beautiful shrine and performed
the funeral rites as though she had buried it
there. But in truth she took the fragments with
her ; and when, after long wanderings, she had
found all, by the mighty power of her magic she
united them again as one body. For when Horus
the Child should be grown to manhood, then he
should fight with Set and avenge his father ; and
after he had obtained the victory Osiris should
live again.

But until that day Osiris lives in the Duat,

where he rules the Dead wisely and nobly as he ruled the living when on earth. For though Horus fights with Set and the battles rage furiously, yet the decisive victory is not yet accomplished, and Osiris has never returned to earth again.

VI

THE SCORPIONS OF ISIS

I AM Isis, the great Goddess, the Mistress of Magic
the Speaker of Spells.

I came out of my house which my brother Se
had given to me, for Thoth called to me to come
Thoth the twice great, mighty of truth in cart'
and in heaven. He called, and I came fort
when Ra descended in glory to the western horizo
of heaven, and it was evening.

And with me came the seven scorpions, an
their names were Tefen and Befen, Mestet an
Mestetef, Petet, Thetet, and Matet. Behind m
were Tefen and Befen ; on either side were Mesto
and Mestetef ; in front were Petet, Thetet, an
Matet, clearing the way that none should oppos
or hinder me. I called aloud to the scorpion
and my words rang through the air and entere
into their ears, " Beware of the Black One, ca
not the Red One, look neither at children nor a
any small helpless creature."

Then I wandered through the Land of Egyp
Tefen and Befen behind me, Mestet and Mestet

52

on either side of me, Petet, Thetet, and Matet
before me ; and we came to Per-sui, where the
crocodile is God, and to the Town of the Two
Sandals, which is the city of the Twin Goddesses.
Here it is that the swamps and marshes of the
North Country begin, where there are fields of
papyrus-reeds, and where the marshmen dwell;
from here to the Great Green Waters is the North
Land.

Then we came near houses where the marsh-
people dwelt, and the name of one of the women
was " Glory," though some called her " Strength "
also. She stood at her door, and from afar she
saw me coming, wayworn and weary, and I would
fain have sat me down in her house to rest.   But
when I would have spoken to her, she shut the
door in my face, for she feared the seven scorpions
that were with me.

I went farther, and one of the marshwomen
opened her door to me, and in her house I rested.
But Mestet and Mestetef, Petet, Thetet, and Matet,
and Befen also, they came together and laid their
poison upon the sting of Tefen ; thus the sting of
Tefen had sevenfold power.   Then returned Tefen
to the house of the woman Glory, she who had
closed her door against me ; the door was still
shut, but between it and the threshold was a
narrow space.   Through this narrow space crept
Tefen and entered the house, and stung with a
sting of sevenfold power the son of the woman

Glory. So fierce and burning was the poison th
the child died and fire broke out in the house.

Then the woman Glory cried and lamented, b
no man hearkened to her, and Heaven its
sent water upon her house. A great marvel w
this water from Heaven, for the time of tl
inundation was not yet.

Thus she mourned and lamented, and h
heart was full of sorrow when she remembered ho
she had shut her door in my face when, weary a1
wayworn, I would have rested in her house. A1
the sound of her grief came to my ears, and 1
heart swelled with sorrow for her sorrow, and
turned back and went with her to where her de
child lay.

And I, Isis, the Mistress of magic, whose voic
can awake the dead, I called aloud the Words ʿ
Power, the Words that even the dead can hea
And I laid my arms upon the child that I migʰ
bring back Life to the lifeless. Cold and still ʰ
lay, for the sevenfold poison of Tefen was in hin
Then did I speak magical spells to the poison ʿ
the scorpions, saying, " O poison of Tefen, com
out of him and fall upon the ground ! Poison ʿ
Befen, advance not, penetrate no farther, com
out of him, and fall upon the ground ! For I a1
Isis, the great Enchantress, the Speaker of spells
Fall down, O poison of Mestet ! Hasten no1
poison of Mestetef ! Rise not, poison of Pete
and Thetet ! Approach not, poison of Matet

For I am Isis, the great Enchantress, the Speaker of spells. The child shall live, the poison shall die! As Horus is strong and well for me, his mother, so shall this child be strong and well for his mother!"

Then the child recovered, and the fire was quenched, and the rain from heaven ceased. And the woman Glory brought all her wealth, her bracelets and her neck-ornaments, her gold-work and silver-work, to the house of the marshwoman, and laid them at my feet in token of repentance that she had shut the door upon me when, weary and wayworn, I had come to her house.

And to this day men make dough of wheat-flour kneaded with salt and lay it upon the wound made by the sting of a scorpion, and over it they recite the Words of Power which I recited over the child of the woman Glory when the sevenfold poison was in him. For I am Isis, the great Enchantress, the Mistress of magic, the Speaker of spells.

VII

THE BLACK PIG

THE reason why the city of Pé was given to Horus, I know and I will tell you.

Between Horus and Set there is enmity and hatred, war and battle. Ever the fight goes on and the combatants rage furiously, and victory is not yet declared to either, though the Gods are with Horus.

Now Set is cunning and crafty, and seeks to conquer by subtlety rather than by courage and skill in the fray; and such power is his that he can take what form he will and deceive both men and Gods. This is the power of Set, but the power of Horus is not the same; for to Horus belong righteousness and truth; deceit and falsehood are not in him. Whoso gazes into the blue eyes of Horus can see the future reflected there, and both Gods and men seek Horus to learn what shall come to pass.

It came to the knowledge of Set that Ra would consult with Horus, and it seemed to him that an opportunity was at hand to injure Horus, so

he took upon himself the form of a Black Pig.
Fierce was his aspect, long and sharp his tushes,
and his colour was the blackness of the thundercloud ; savage and evil was his look, and struck
fear into the hearts of men.

Then came the Majesty of Ra to Horus and
spoke to him saying, " Let me look in thine eyes
and behold what is to come." And he gazed into
the eyes of Horus, and their colour was that of
the Great Green Waters when the summer sky
shines upon them. And while he gazed, the Black
Pig passed by.

Ra knew not that it was the Evil God, and he
cried out to Horus and said, " Look at that Black
Pig ! Never have I seen one so huge and so fierce."

And Horus looked ; neither did he know Set
in this strange form, and thought it was a wild
boar from the thickets of the North Country.
Thus he was off his guard and unprotected against
his enemy.

Then Set aimed a blow of fire at the eye of
Horus, and Horus shouted aloud with the pain
of the fire, and raged furiously, and cried, " It
is Set, and he has smitten me with fire on the
eyes."

But Set was no longer there, for he had con-
veyed himself away, and the Black Pig was seen no
more. And Ra cursed the pig because of Set, and
said, " Let the pig be an abomination to Horus."
And to this day men sacrifice the pig when the

Moon is at the full, because Set, the enemy (
Horus, and the murderer of Osiris, took its forr
in order to injure the blue-eyed God. And fc
this reason also swineherds are unclean througl
out the land of Egypt ; never may they ente
the temples and sacrifice to the Gods, and the
sons and daughters may not marry with th
worshippers of the Gods.

And when the eyes of Horus were healed, R
gave to him the city of Pé, and he gave to hii
two divine brethren in the city of Pé, and tw
divine brethren in the city of Nekhen to be wit
him as everlasting judges. Then was the heai
of Horus glad and he rejoiced, and at the joy (
Horus the earth blossomed, and thundercloud
and rain were blotted out.

VIII

THE BATTLES OF HORUS

It was in the three hundred and sixty-third year of the reign of the God Ra-Horakhti upon earth that the great war happened between Horus and Set.

The Majesty of the God Ra, whom men call Ra-Horakhti also, was in Nubia with his army, a great and innumerable multitude of soldiers, footmen and horsemen, archers and chariots. He came in his Boat upon the river; the prow ·of the Boat was of palm-wood, its stern was of acacia-wood, and he landed at Thest-Hor, to the east of the Inner Waters. And to him came Horus of Edfu, he whose name is Harpooner and Hero, seeking for that Wicked One, Set, the murderer of Osiris. Long had he sought, but Set had ever eluded him.

The Majesty of Ra had gathered his forces, for Set had rebelled against him, and Horus was glad at the thought of battle, for he loved an hour of fighting more than a day of rejoicing. He entered into the presence of Thoth, the twice great, god

59

of magic, and Thoth gave him the power to change himself into a great winged disk, a disk that glowed like a ball of fire, with great wings on either side like the colours of the sky at sunset when the blue shades from dark to light, and is shot with gold and flame. Men try to copy these hues when they carve the winged disk above the temple-doors, or make it into a breast-ornament of gold inlaid with turquoise and carnelian and lazuli.

Thus Horus, as a great winged disk, sat on the prow of the Boat of Ra, and his splendour flashed across the waters and fell upon his foes as they lay in ambush. Upon his glorious wings he rose into the air, and against his crafty enemies he made a curse, a curse terrible and fear-striking, saying, " Your eyes shall be blinded, and ye shall not see ; and your ears shall be deaf, and ye shall not hear."

And at once, when each man looked at his neighbour, he saw a stranger ; and when he heard his own familiar mother-tongue it sounded like a foreign language, and they cried out that they were betrayed, and that the enemy had come among them. They turned their weapons each against the other, and in the quickness of a moment many had ceased to live, and the rest had fled, while over them flew the gleaming Disk watching for Set. But Set was in the marshes of the North Country and these were but his advance-guard.

Then Horus flew back to Ra, and Ra embraced him and gave him a draught of wine mixed with water. And to this day men pour a libation of wine and water to Horus at this place in remembrance. When Horus had drunk the wine, he spoke to the Majesty of Ra and said, " Come and see thine enemies, how they lie overthrown in their blood." Ra came, and with him came Astarte, Mistress of Horses, driving her furious steeds ; and they saw the corpse-strewn field where the army of Set had slain one another.

Now this is the first encounter in the South, but the last great battle was not yet.

Then the associates of Set came together and took counsel, and took upon themselves the likeness of crocodiles and hippopotamuses, for these great beasts can live under water and no human weapon can pierce their hides. They came up the river, the water swirling behind them, and rushed upon the Boat of Ra to overturn it. But Horus had gathered together his band of armourers and weapon-smiths, and they had prepared arrows and spears of metal, smelted and welded, hammered and shaped, with magical words and spells chanted over them. When the fierce beasts came up the river in waves of foam, the Followers of Horus drew their bowstrings and let fly their arrows, they cast their javelins, and charged with their spears. And the metal pierced the hides and reached the hearts, and o these wicked animals six hundred and fifty were slain, and the rest fled.

Now this is the second encounter in the South, but the last great battle was not yet.

The associates of Set fled, some up the river and some down the river ; their hearts were weak and their feet failed for fear of Horus, the Harpooner, the Hero. And those whose faces were towards the South Land fled fastest, for Horus was at their back in the Boat of Ra ; and with him came his Followers, their weapons in their hands.

At the south-east of Denderah, the city of Hathor, Horus saw the enemy, and he rushed upon them with his Followers, while Ra and Thoth watched the conflict as they waited in the Boat.

Then said the Majesty of Ra to Thoth, " See, how he wounds his enemies ! See, how Horus of Edfu carries destruction among them ! " And afterwards men built a shrine in this place in remembrance of the fight, and the Gods in the shrine were Ra and Min and Horus of Edfu.

Now this is the third encounter in the South, but the last great battle was not yet.

Then quickly they turned the Boat, and swiftly was it carried downstream, following the fugitives, whose faces were towards the North Land. For a night and a day they followed after, and at the north-east of Denderah Horus saw them. And he made haste, he and his Followers, and fell

upon them, and slew them. Great and terrible
was the slaughter as he drove them before him.

Thus was destroyed Set's army in the South
in four great encounters, but the last great battle
was not yet.

Now the allies of Set turned their faces towards
the lake and towards the marshes of the sea.
Horus came behind them in the Boat of Ra, and
his form was the form of a great winged disk ; and
with him came his Followers, their weapons in
their hands. Then Horus commanded silence,
and silence was upon their mouths.

Four days and four nights were they upon the
water seeking the enemy. But none did they
find, for their foes had turned their shapes into
the shapes of crocodiles and hippopotamuses, and
lay hidden in the water. On the morning of the
fifth day Horus saw them ; at once he gave battle,
and the air was filled with the noise of the combat,
while Ra and Thoth watched the conflict as they
waited in the Boat.

Then the Majesty of Ra cried aloud when he
saw Horus like a devouring flame upon the battle-
field, "See, how he casts his weapon against them,
he kills them, he destroys them with his sword,
he cuts them in pieces, he utterly defeats them !
See and behold Horus of Edfu ! " At the end
of the fight Horus came back in triumph and he
brought one hundred and forty-two prisoners to
the Boat of Ra.

Now this is the first encounter in the North, t
the last great battle was not yet.

For the enemies, who were upon the Northe
Waters, turned their faces towards the ca
to reach the sea, and they came to the Weste
Waters of Mert, where the Ally of Set had
dwelling. Behind them followed Horus, equip
with all his glittering weapons, and he went in t
Boat of Ra, and Ra was in the Boat with eight
his train. They were upon the Northern Car
and backwards and forwards they went, turn
and re-turning, but nothing did they see or he
Then they went northward for a night and a d
and they came to the House of Rerhu.

There Ra spoke to Horus and said, "Beho
thy enemies are gathered together at the West
Waters of Mert, where dwell the Allies of Se
And Horus of Edfu prayed the Majesty of Ra
come in his Boat against the Allies of Set.

Again they travelled to the northwards, wh
the never-setting Stars wheel round a certain po
in the sky, and on the banks of the Western Wat
of Mert were the Allies of Set, ready for bat
Then Horus of Edfu delayed not a moment,
rushed upon the foe, and with him came
Followers, their weapons in their hands. De
and destruction they dealt to right and to
till the enemy fled before them. When the c
flict was over, they counted the prisoners ; th
hundred and eighty-one were taken, and th

Horus slew before the Boat of Ra, and their weapons he gave to his Followers.

Now this is the second encounter in the North, but the last great battle was not yet.

And now, at last, Set himself came forth from his hiding-place. Fierce and savage he is, cunning and cruel; in his nature like a beast of prey, without ruth or pity; and men make his image with the head of a wild beast, for human feeling is to him unknown. From his hiding-place he came forth and he roared terribly. The earth and the heavens trembled at the sound of his roaring and at the words which he uttered, for he boasted that he would himself fight against Horus and destroy him as he had destroyed Osiris.

The wind bore the words of his boasting to Ra, and Ra said to Thoth the twice great, Lord of Magic and Wisdom, " Cause that these high words of the Terrible One be cast down."

Then Horus of Edfu sprang forward and rushed at his enemy, and a great fight raged. Horus cast his weapon and killed many, and his Followers fought also and prevailed. Out of the dust and the noise of the combat came Horus, dragging a prisoner; and the captive's arms were bound behind him, and the staff of Horus was tied across his mouth so that he could make no sound, and the weapon of Horus was at his throat.

Horus dragged him before the Majesty of Ra. And Ra spoke and said to Horus, " Do with him

5

as thou wilt." Then Horus fell upon his enemy
and struck the weapon into his head and into h
back, and cut off his head, and dragged the bod
about by the feet, and at last he cut the body int
pieces. Thus did he treat the body of his adve·
sary as Set had treated the body of Osiris. Th
took place on the seventh day of the first mont
of the season when the earth appears after tl
inundation. And the lake is called the Lake (
Fighting to this day.

Now this is the third encounter in the Nortl
but the last great battle was not yet.

For it was the Ally of Set whom Horus ha
slain, and Set himself was still alive, and he rage
against Horus as a panther of the South. An
he stood up and roared in the face of heaven, an
his voice was the voice of thunder, and as 1
ᵣroared he changed himself into a great snake, an
·entered into the earth. None saw him go an
none saw him change, but he was fighting again:
the Gods, and by their power and knowledge a:
they aware of what comes to pass, though no ma
tells them. And Ra said to Horus, "Set h«
transformed himself into a hissing snake and h«
entered the earth. We must cause that he nev(
comes forth ; never, never no more ! "

The associates of Set took courage, knowir
that their leader was alive, and they assemble
again, and their boats filled the canal. The Boa
of Ra went against them, and above the Boa

shone the glory of the great winged Disk.   When Horus saw the enemy gathered together in one place, he drove at them and routed them and slew them without number.

Now this is the fourth encounter in the North, but the last great battle was not yet.

Then Horus of Edfu remained in the Boat of Ra upon the canal for six days and six nights, watching for the enemy, but he saw none, for they lay as corpses in the water.

And to this day men make ceremonies in remembrance of the Battles of Horus on the first day of the first month of the inundation, on the seventh day of the first month of the appearing of the earth after the inundation, and on the twenty-first and twenty-fourth days of the second month of the earth's appearing.   These days are kept holy at Ast-abt, which is at the south side of Anrudef, where is one of the graves of Osiris.   And Isis made magical spells round Anrudef that no enemy might come near it ; and the priestess of Anrudef is called "The Lady of Spells" to this day in remembrance ; and the waters are called "The Waters of Seeking," for there it was that Horus sought for his foe.

And Horus sent out his Followers, and they hunted down the enemy, and brought in prisoners ; one hundred and six from the East and one hundred and six from the West.   These they slew before Ra in the sanctuaries.

Then Ra gave to Horus and his fighters tw
cities which are called the Mesen-cities to this da
for the Followers of Horus are Mesenti, the Meta
workers.   In the shrines of the Mesen-cities Hor
is the God, and his secret ceremonies are held ᴄ
four days in the year.   Great and holy are the
days in the Mesen-cities, for they are in reme
brance of the Battles of Horus which he foug
against Set, the murderer of Osiris.

Now these enemies, they gathered again in t
East, and they travelled towards Tharu.   Th
was launched the Boat of Ra to follow after the
and Horus of Edfu transformed himself into t
likeness of a lion with the face of a man ; his arn
were like flint, and on his head was the Atef-crown
which is the white diadem of the South Land wit
feathers and horns, and on either side a crowne
serpent.   And he hastened after his enemies, an
defeated them, and brought of prisoners on
hundred and forty-two.

Then said Ra to Horus of Edfu, " Let us journe
northwards to the Great Green Waters, and smit
the foe there as we have smitten him in Egypt.

Northwards they went, and the enemy fle
before them, and they reached the Great Gree
Waters, where the waves broke on the shoɪ
with the noise of thunder.   Then Thoth arose an
he stood in the midst of the Boat, and he chante
strange words over the boats and barges of Horu
and his Followers, and the sea fell calm as th

sound of the words floated across its waves. And there was silence on the Great Green Waters, for the wind was lulled, and naught was in sight save the boats of Ra and of Horus.

Then said the Majesty of Ra, " Let us sail round the whole extent of the land, let us sail to the South Land." And they knew that Ra was aware of the enemy. They made haste and sailed to the South Land by night, to the country of Ta-kens, and they came to the town of Shaïs, but until they reached Shaïs they saw naught of any enemy. Now Shaïs is on the border of Nubia, and in Nubia were the guards of the enemy.

Then Horus of Edfu changed himself into a great winged Disk with gleaming pinions outspread, and on either side of him came the goddesses Nekhbet and Uazet, and their form was the form of great hooded snakes with crowns upon their heads ; on the head of Nekhbet was the white crown of the South Land, on the head of Uazet was the red crown of the North Land.

And the Gods in the Boat of Ra cried aloud and said, " See, O Thou who art twice great, he has placed himself between the two goddesses. Behold how he overthrows his adversaries and destroys them."

Now this is the encounter in Nubia, but the last great battle was not yet.

- Then came Ra in his Boat and he moored at Thest-Hor, and he gave commandment that in

every temple throughout the Two Lands men
should carve the Winged Disk, and on the righ
and left of the Disk should be Nekhbet and Uaze
as great hooded snakes with crowns upon thei
heads. And the temple at the point of Thest
Hor is called " The House of Horus in the South '
to this day in remembrance, and a great offerin
is made there to Ra and Horus. And Ra gav
to Horus the province of the House of Fighting
and Ast-Abt, and the Mesen-cities of the Eas
and the West, and Edfu of the North, and Tharu
and Gauti, and the Sea of Sailing, and Uppe
Shasu, and Edfu-of-the-House-of-Ra. And fro
the lake south of Edfu-of-the-House-of-Ra the
bring water to the two Houses of the King on the
day of the Sed-festival. And Isis carried Ar-stone
of sand to Thest-Hor—Ar-stone of the Star was it
and in every place in the South Land to which
Horus went, there is Ar-stone found to this day.

Now some say that the last great battle is stil
to come, and that in the end Horus will kill Set
and that Osiris and all the Gods will reign on earth
when their enemy is utterly destroyed. Bu
others say that the battle is already ended and
that Horus slew the great and wicked Foe who
had wrought misery and calamity to all.

And this is what they say : After months and
years Horus the Child grew to manhood. Then
came Set with his allies, and he challenged Horus
in the presence of Ra. And Horus came forth

his Followers with him in their boats, with their armour, and their glittering weapons with handles of worked wood, and their cords, and their spears.

And Isis made golden ornaments for the prow of the boat of Horus, and she laid them in their places with magic words and spells, saying, " Gold is at the prow of thy boat, O Lord of Mesen, Horus, Chieftain of the boat, the great boat of Horus, the boat of rejoicing. May the valour of Ra, the strength of Shu, power and fear be around thee. Thou art victorious, O son of Osiris, son of Isis, for thou fightest for the throne of thy father."

Then Set took upon himself the form of a red hippopotamus, great and mighty, and he came from the South Land with his Allies, travelling to the North Land to meet Horus of Edfu. And at Elephantine, Set stood up and spoke a great curse against Horus of Edfu and against Isis, and said, " Let there come a great wind, even a furious north-wind and a raging tempest "; and the sound of his voice was like thunder in the East of the sky. His words were cried from the southern heaven and rolled back to the northern heaven, a word and a cry from Set, the enemy of Osiris and the Gods.

At once a storm broke over the boats of Horus and his Followers, the wind roared, and the water was lashed into great waves, and the boats were tossed like straws. But Horus held on his way ;

and through the darkness of the storm and th
foam of the waves gleamed the golden prow lik
the rays of the sun.

And Horus took upon himself the form of a
young man ; his height was eight cubits ; in hi,
hand he held a harpoon, the blade was four cubits,
the shaft twenty cubits, and a chain of sixty cubits
was welded to it.   Over his head he brandished th
weapon as though it were a reed, and he launched
it at the great red hippopotamus which stood
in the deep waters, ready to destroy Horus and
his Followers when the storm should wreck their
boats.

And at the first cast the weapon struck deep into
the head of the great red hippopotamus and
entered the brain.   Thus died Set, that great
and wicked One, the enemy of Osiris and the
Gods.

And to this day the priests of Horus of Edfu,
and the King's daughters, and the women of
Busiris and the women of Pé chant a hymn and
strike the drum for Horus in triumph.

And this is their song : " Rejoice, O women
of Busiris ! Rejoice, O women of Pé ! Horus
has overthrown his enemies !

" Exult, dwellers in Edfu ! Horus, the great
God, Lord of heaven, has smitten the enemy of
his father !

" Eat ye the flesh of the vanquished, drink ye
his blood, burn ye his bones in the flame of the

fire. Let him be cut in pieces, and let his bones be given to the cats, the fragments of him to the reptiles.

"O Horus, the Striker, the great One of Valour, the Slayer, the Chief of the Gods, the Harpooner, the Hero, the only begotten, Captor of captives, Horus of Edfu, Horus the Avenger!

"He has destroyed the wicked One, he has made a whirlpool with the blood of his enemy, his shaft has made a prey. Behold ye, see ye Horus at the prow of his boat. Like Ra, he shines on the horizon. He is decked in green linen, in binding linen, in fine linen and byssus. The double diadem is upon thy head, the two serpents upon thy brow, O Horus the Avenger!

"Thy harpoon is of metal, the shaft is of the sycomore of the desert, the net is woven by Hathor of the Roses. Thou hast aimed to the right, thou hast cast to the left. We give praise to thee to the height of heaven, for thou hast chained the wickedness of thine enemy. We give praise to thee, we worship thy majesty, O Horus of Edfu, Horus the Avenger!"

IX

THE BEER OF HELIOPOLIS

Now the Majesty of Ra reigned over the Tw
Lands. He was the second king of Egypt, an
in his reign peace was on earth, and harvest
were so plentiful that to this day men speak c
the good things which "happened in the tim
of Ra." By his own power he created himsel
and he created heaven and earth, gods and me
and he ruled over them all.

For hundreds and hundreds of years he rule
until he waxed old, and men no longer feared hi
but laughed and said, "Look at Ra! He is ol
his bones are like silver, his flesh like gold, a
his hair like true lapis lazuli."

Then Ra was wroth when he heard their jes
and their laughter, and he called to those wl
were in his train, "Summon hither my daughte
the apple of my eye, and summon also the go
Shu and Tefnut, Geb and Nut, and the gre
god Nun, whose dwelling is in the waters of tl
sky. Do my bidding secretly lest men shou

hear you and see you, for then would they be afraid and hide themselves."

In secret went the messengers, very softly they came to summon the gods and goddesses. Secretly and softly came the gods and goddesses to the Mansion of Ra in the Hidden Place. Naught did men see or hear; and they laughed again at Ra, not knowing the punishment that should fall upon them.

On each side of the throne came the gods and goddesses, and they bowed before the Majesty of Ra with their foreheads to the ground, saying, " Speak that we may hear."

Then said Ra to Nun, the great god whose dwelling is in the waters of the sky, " O eldest of the gods and all ye ancestor-gods! Behold the men whom I have created, how they speak against me. Tell me what ye would that I should do to them, for verily I will not slay them till I have heard your words."

And Nun, the great god whose dwelling is in the waters of the sky, made answer, " My son Ra, greatest of gods, mightiest of kings, thy throne is set fast, and thy fear will be upon all the world when thou sendest out thy daughter, the apple of thine eye, against those who attack thee."

The Majesty of Ra spoke again, " Lo, they will flee to the deserts and the mountains and hide themselves, if fear falls upon their hearts

on account of their jests and laughter; and '
the deserts and mountains none can find them.'

Then said the gods and goddesses, bowing b
fore him with their foreheads on the groun
" Send forth thy daughter, the apple of thine ey
against them."

And at once there came the daughter of R
Sekhmet is she called, and Hathor, fiercest of tl
goddesses; like a lion she rushes on her pre
slaughter is her delight, and her pleasure is i
blood.

At her father's bidding she entered the Tw
Lands to slay those who had rebelled against t
Majesty of Ra, and had turned their rebellio
to jest and laughter. In the land of Ta-mer
she killed them, and on the mountains which li
to the east and west of the great river. To an
fro she hastened, slaying all who crossed he
path, and before her fled the rebels against Ra.

And Ra looked forth upon the earth and crie
to his daughter, the apple of his eye, " Come i
peace, O Hathor! Hast thou done that whic
I gave thee to do ? "

And Hathor laughed as she answered, and he
laugh was the terrible voice of the lioness as sh
tears her prey. " By thy life, O Ra," she criec
" I work my will upon men, and my heart re
joices."

For many nights the river ran red, and th
goddess waded in the blood of men, and her fee

were red as she strode through the land of Egypt as far as Henen-seten.

Then Ra looked forth upon the earth again, and his heart was filled with pity for men, though they had rebelled against him. But none could stop the ruthless goddess, not even the Majesty of Ra himself ; of herself must she cease to slay, for neither gods nor men could compel her. By subtlety alone could this be accomplished.

Ra gave command, saying, " Call hither to me messengers who are swift as the blast of the storm wind." And when they were brought, he said, " Run to Elephantine, hasten, go quickly, and bring back to me the fruit that causes sleep. Be swift, be swift, for all this must be accomplished ere the day dawn."

The messengers hastened, and their speed was the speed of a blast of the storm-wind. They came to Elephantine, where the great river rages among the rocks that bar its passage ; they took the fruit that causes sleep, and with the fleetness of the wind they brought it to Ra. Crimson and scarlet was the fruit, and its juice was the colour of man's blood ; and the messengers carried to it Heliopolis, the city of Ra.

Then the women of Heliopolis crushed barley and made beer, and with the beer they mixed the juice of the fruit that causes sleep, and the beer became the colour of blood. Seven thousand measures of beer did they make, and in haste they brewed it, for the night was drawing to close and the day was about to break. In ha, came the Majesty of Ra, and all the gods a goddesses, who were with him, to Heliopc to inspect the beer. Ra saw that it was li human blood, and he said, "Very good is t beer. By this I can protect mankind."

At the dawning of the day, he gave comma "Carry this beer to the place where men a women have been slain, and pour it out upon t fields before the beauty of the night has passe So they poured it out upon the fields. Fo palms deep it lay upon the ground, and its colo was the colour of blood.

In the morning came the fierce Sekhmet, reac to slay, and as she passed by she looked to tl side and that, watching for her prey. But i living thing did she see, only the fields that l four palms deep in the beer that was the colo of blood. Then she laughed with the laugh li: the roar of a lioness, for she thought it was t blood she had shed. And she stooped and dran Again and again she drank, and she laughed tl more, for the juice of the fruit that causes sle(mounted to her brain, and no longer could sl see to slay by reason of the juice of that fruit.

Then the Majesty of Ra said to her, "Con in peace, O sweet one." And to this day tl maidens of Amu are called "Sweet Ones" remembrance.

And the Majesty of Ra spoke again to the goddess, saying, " For thee shall be prepared drinks from the fruits that cause sleep; every year shall these be made at the great Festival of the New Year, and the number of them shall be according to the number of the priestesses who serve me."

And to this day, on the festival of Hathor, drinks are made of the fruits that cause sleep, according to the number of the priestesses of Ra, in remembrance of the protection of mankind from the fury of the goddess.

X

THE NAME OF RA

Now the Majesty of Ra was the creator of hea
and earth, of gods, men, and cattle, of fire, and t
breath of life ; and he ruled over gods and m
And Isis saw his might, the might that reac
over heaven and earth, before which all g
and men bowed ; and she longed in her he
for that power, that thereby she should
greater than the gods and have dominion ov
men.

There was but one way to obtain that pow
By the knowledge of his own name did Ra ru
and none but himself knew that secret nan
Whosoever could learn the secret, to that o
—god or man—would belong the dominion ov
all the world, and even Ra himself must be
subjection. Jealously did Ra guard his secr
and kept it ever in his breast, lest it should
taken from him, and his power diminished.

Every morning Ra came forth in his glory
the head of his train from the horizon of t
East, journeying across the sky, and in t

evening they came to the horizon of the West, and the Majesty of Ra sank in his glory to lighten the thick darkness of the Duat. Many, many times had Ra made the journey, so many times that now he had waxed old. Very aged was Ra, and the saliva ran down from his mouth and fell upon the earth.

Then Isis took earth and mixed it with the saliva, and she kneaded the clay and moulded it, and formed it into the shape of a snake, the shape of the great hooded snake that is the emblem of all goddesses, the royal serpent which is upon the brow of the Kings of Egypt. No charms or magic spells did she use, for in the snake was the divine substance of Ra himself. She took the snake and laid it hidden in the path of Ra, the path on which he travelled in journeying from the eastern to the western horizon of heaven.

In the morning came Ra and his train in their glory journeying to the western horizon of heaven, where they enter the Duat and lighten the thick darkness. And the serpent shot out its pointed head which was shaped like a dart, and its fangs sank into the flesh of Ra, and the fire of its poison entered into the God, for the divine substance was in the serpent.

Ra cried aloud, and his cry rang through the heavens from the eastern to the western horizon ; across the earth it rang, and gods and men alike heard the cry of Ra. And the gods who follow

6

in his train said to him, "What aileth the
What aileth thee ? "

But Ra answered never a word, he trembled
all his limbs, and his teeth chattered, and nau[
did he say, for the poison spread over his bc
as Hapi spreads over the land, when the wat
rise above their banks at the time of the ov
flowing of the river.

When he had become calm, he called to th
who followed him and said, "Come to me, ye wh
I created. I am hurt by a grievous thing. I f
it, though I see it not, neither is it the creatior
my hands, and I know not who has made
Never, never have I felt pain like this, nev
never has there been an injury worse than t
Who can hurt me ? For none know my sec
name, that name which was spoken by my fat
and by my mother, and hidden in me that n
might work witchcraft upon me. I came fo
to look upon the world which I had made
passed across the Two Lands when somethin
I know not what—struck me. Is it fire ? I[
water ? I burn, I shiver, I tremble in all
limbs. Call to me the children of the gods, t]
who have skill in healing, they who have kn
ledge of magic, they whose power reaches
heaven."

Then came all the gods with weeping and mou
ing and lamentations ; their power was of no a
against the serpent, for in it the divine substa

was incorporated. With them came Isis the Healer, the Mistress of Magic, in whose mouth is the Breath of Life, whose words destroy disease and awake the dead.

She spoke to the Majesty of Ra and said. " What is this, O divine Father ? what is this ? Has a snake brought pain to thee ? Has the creation of thy hand lifted up its head against thee ? Lo, it shall be overthrown by the might of my magic, I will drive it out by means of thy glory."

Then the Majesty of Ra answered, " I passed along the appointed path, I crossed over the Two Lands, when a serpent that I saw not struck me with its fangs. Was it fire ? Was it water ? I am colder than water, I am hotter than fire, I tremble in all my limbs, and the sweat runs down my face as down the faces of men in the fierce heat of summer."

And Isis spoke again, and her voice was low and soothing, " Tell me thy Name, O divine Father, thy true Name, thy secret Name, for he only can live who is called by his name."

Then the Majesty of Ra answered, " I am the Maker of heaven and earth, I am the Establisher of the mountains, I am the Creator of the waters, I am the Maker of the secrets of the two Horizons, I am Light and I am Darkness, I am the Maker of Hours, the Creator of Days, I am the Opener of Festivals, I am the Maker of running streams,

I am the Creator of living flame. I am Khepe
in the morning, Ra at noontide, and Atmu in t
evening."

But Isis held her peace ; never a word did s
speak, for she knew that Ra had told her t
names that all men know ; his true Name,]
secret Name, was still hidden in his breast. A
the power of the poison increased, and ran throu
his veins like burning flame.

After a silence she spoke again. " Thy Nan
thy true Name, thy secret Name, was not amo
those. Tell me thy Name that the poison m
be driven out, for only he whose name I kn
can be healed by the might of my magic." A
the power of the poison increased, and the p
was as the pain of living fire.

Then the Majesty of Ra cried out and sa
" Let Isis come with me, and let my Name p
from my breast to her breast."

And he hid himself from the gods that follow
in his train. Empty was the Boat of the S
empty was the great throne of the God, for
had hidden himself from his Followers and fr
the creations of his hands.

When the Name came forth from the heart
Ra to pass to the heart of Isis, the goddess sp
to Ra and said, " Bind thyself with an oath
Ra, that thou wilt give thy two eyes unto Hori
Now the two Eyes of Ra are the sun and the mo
and men call them the Eyes of Horus to this d

Thus was the Name of Ra taken from him and given to Isis, and she, the great Enchantress, cried aloud the Word of Power, and the poison obeyed, and Ra was healed by the might of his Name.

And Isis, the great One, Mistress of the Gods, Mistress of magic, she is the skilful Healer, in her mouth is the Breath of Life, by her words she destroys pain, and by her power she awakes the dead.

XI

THE REGIONS OF NIGHT AND THICI DARKNESS

WHEN the world came into being, there were tw rivers, the river of Egypt and the river of tl sky. Great is the Nile, the river of Egypt, risii in his two caverns in the South beyond tl cataract, flooding the land of Egypt and bringii joy and good harvests to Ta-mery. Great al mighty is the river of the sky, flowing across t heavens and through the Duat, the world night and of thick darkness, and on that riv floats the Boat of Ra. Boat of Millions of Yea is its name, but men call it the Manzet Boat the dawn, when Ra rises in splendour on t eastern horizon of heaven ; the Mesektet Bo is it called in the evening, when Ra enters in glo within the portals of the Duat, where the mou tain of Manu lifts its peaks to the western sk On the western horizon is the mountain of Man and on the eastern horizon the mountain Bakhu ; vast and huge are they, raising th crests above the earth, and the sky rests up

their summits. And on the topmost peak of the
mountain of Bakhu dwells a serpent; thirty
cubits in length is he, and his scales are of flint
and of glittering metal. He guards the mountain
and the Great Green Waters, and none can pass
by him save Ra in his Boat.

In the evening Ra descends in majesty to the
Western horizon of heaven, to the portals of
the Duat at the Gap of Abydos. Splendid is the
Mesektet Boat, glorious its trappings, and its
colours are of amethyst and emerald, jasper and
turquoise, lazuli and the lustre of gold. At the
Gap of Abydos waits a company of gods to prepare
the Boat for the journey through the Duat, the
land of night and of thick darkness. Stripped is
the Boat of its splendour, bare and without glory
is it when it passes through the portals of the Duat,
and in it is the body of Ra, lifeless and dead.

Then the gods take the great towing-ropes;
slowly the Boat moves along the river. The
portals of the Duat are flung wide, and the twelve
goddesses of the night take their place upon the
Boat to guide it through the gloom and perils
of the Duat; pilots of the river are they, and
without them not Ra himself could pass through
unscathed.

" Watercourse of Ra " is the name of the first
country of the Duat. Sombre is this land, yet not
wholly dark ; for on either side the river are six
serpents, coiled and with heads erect, and the

breath of their mouths is a flame of fire. In tl
cabin of the Boat is Ra, dead and lifeless;
the prow are Up-uaut, the Opener of the Way
and Sa, and the goddess of the hour. Round abou
the cabin are a company of gods ; these are the
who guard Ra from all perils and dangers, an
from the attack of the abominable Apep.

Slowly goes the Boat of Ra, passing throug
the Duat, to regions of thick darkness, of horr
and dismay, where the dead have their habitation
and Apep lies in wait for the coming of R.
Thus passes the first hour of the night, and tl
second hour is at hand.

At the entrance of every country of the Du
is a gate ; tall are the walls, and narrow is t
passage ; upon the walls are spearheads, sha
and pointed, that no man may climb over. T
door of the gate is of wood, turning on a piv
and a monstrous snake guards the door. Nc
may pass by him save those only to whom
name is known. At the turn of the passage a
two great hooded snakes, the one above, t
other below. The breath of their mouths is fi
and poison mingled ; through the narrow port
on every side they send forth streams of flai
and venom. At either end of the passage stan
a warder, keeping watch.

Then the goddess of the first hour makes w
for the goddess of the second hour, and she ca
aloud the name of the Guardian of the ga

Flung wide are the portals, the fire and poison cease, and the Boat of Ra passes through.

" Ur-nes " do we name this second country of the Duat, but the Hanebu and those who inhabit the isles of the Great Green Waters call it Ouranos. The river is wide and bears on its dark waters four shallops ; no oars have they, neither masts nor rudders, but float upon the stream and are carried by the current. Mysterious and strange are they, and the shadowy shapes which fill them have forms like the forms of men.   In this country Ra is Lord and King, and those who live here are in peace, for none can pass the great hooded snakes who guard the gates, whose breath is mingled flame and venom.   Happy are those who inhabit this land, for here dwell the spirits of the corn, Besa and Nepra and Tepu-yn.   These are they who make the wheat and barley to flourish and cause the fruits of the earth to increase.

Slowly goes the Boat of Ra, passing through the Duat, through regions of thick darkness, of horror and dismay, where the dead have their habitation, and Apep lies in wait for the coming of Ra.   Thus passes the second hour of the night, and the third hour is at hand.   Then the goddess of the second hour makes way for the goddess of the third hour, and she calls aloud the name of the Guardian of the gate.   Flung wide are the portals, and the Boat of Ra passes through.

" Watercourse of the only God " is the name of

the third country of the Duat, and here in tl
beautiful Amentet is the Kingdom of Osiris. (
either side the river are the great shapes of tl
gods surrounding the form of Osiris himse
Enthroned is he, appearing in splendour as kin
with the White Crown of the South Land ai
the Red Crown of the North Land upon his head

Great is Osiris, god of the dead, for all who d
come before him for judgment, and their hear
are weighed in the balance against the feather
Truth. His throne is set upon a running strean
clear and deep, and from the waters rises a sing
lotus-blossom, the colour of the sky at mornin
Upon the blossom stand the four Children
Horus, they who assist Osiris at the Judgmen
who protect the bodies of the dead. To the
belong the South and the North, the West ai
the East, and the four great goddesses are th
protectors. They stand upon the lotus-blosso
and their faces are towards Osiris ; the first h
the face of a man, the second the face of an a
the third the face of a jackal, and the fourth t
face of a bird of prey. This is the hour whi
evil-doers fear ; by their own actions are th
judged, and naught can avail them. Heavy
the heart of the evil-doer and drags down t
scale ; lower and lower it sinks till it reaches t
jaws of Amemt, the Devourer of Hearts. Th
is the evil-doer driven forth into the thick dar
ness of the Duat, to dwell with the abomina

Apep and to fall at last into the Pits of Fire.

But some there are who have wrought righteousness upon earth ; who have hurt no man by fraud or violence ; who have succoured the widow, the orphan, and the shipwrecked mariner ; who have given food to the hungry and clothes to the naked ; who have not stirred up strife, nor caused the shedding of tears. When these come to the Judgment of Osiris, and their hearts are put in the balance, then is the feather of Truth the heavier. The scale with the feather sinks down, and the scale with the heart rises up. Then does Thoth, the twice-great, take the heart and place it again in the breast of the man, and Horus takes him by the hand and leads him to the foot of the throne of Osiris that he may dwell in the kingdom of Osiris for ever and for evermore. And now only can he see the most pure and truly holy Osiris, for " the souls of men are not able to participate of the divine nature whilst they are encompassed about with bodies and passions. . . . When they are freed from these impediments and remove into those purer and unseen regions . . . 'tis then that this God becomes their Leader and King ; upon him they wholly depend, still beholding without satiety, and still ardently longing after that beauty, which 'tis not possible for man to express or think." *

* Plutarch, *De Iside et Osiride* (Squire's translation).

Slowly goes the Boat of Ra, passing throu
the Duat, to regions of thick darkness, of hor
and dismay, where the abominable Apep lies
wait for the coming of Ra, and where the Pits
Fire are prepared for the wicked. Thus pas
the third hour of the night, and the fourth h
is at hand. Then the goddess of the third h
makes way for the goddess of the fourth ho
and she calls aloud the name of the Guard
of the gate. Flung wide are the portals, and
Boat of Ra passes through.

" Living one of forms " is the name of the fou
country of the Duat, and Sokar has domin
in this land. Dreary is the waste of sand, limitl
the desert, gloomy and sombre the landscape. I
blade of grass is seen, no tree, no herbage ; naug
grows, naught lives, save monstrous many-head
serpents, gliding along the ground or creeping up
legs. Terrible are they of aspect as they writ
and turn and hiss and roar ; they raise th
hideous crests on high and hold their dusky wir
outspread. But their anger is not towards F
and he passes safely through their midst.

Engulfed is the great river and lost benea
the shifting sands, and where it ran is now a de
ravine. The walls of rock rise high and ste
and ever the way winds and turns between t
rocks. Men call this place Re-stau, the Mou
of the Tomb. Even in this gloomy desert Osi
has dominion ; Lord of Re-stau is he called, the

fore none need fear when traversing the narrow path. And now the Boat of Ra can no longer float upon the water, but is changed into a great and mighty serpent with glittering scales. At the prow is a serpent's head with eyes watchful and fierce, at the stern is a serpent's head with poison-fangs prepared. Over the sand it glides as a boat glides over the water.

Slowly goes the Boat of Ra, passing through the Duat, through regions of thick darkness, of horror and dismay, to the place where Apep lies in wait for the coming of Ra. Thus passes the fourth hour of the night, and the fifth hour is at hand. Then the goddess of the fourth hour makes way for the goddess of the fifth hour, and she calls aloud the name of the Guardian of the gate. Flung wide are the portals, and the Boat of Ra passes through.

"Hidden" is the name of the fifth country of the Duat, and in this dark and gloomy region dwells Sokar, its Lord and King, god of those who are buried. Beside a turn of the winding way is his dwelling deep below the ground ; above it rises a high mountain of sand. Guarding it on either side are two sphinxes ; lions are they in their bodies, with the faces of men ; and their claws are outstretched like the talons of a beast of prey. In the midst lies a serpent with three heads, and between his wings stands Sokar in the form of a man with the head of a hawk. Savage and fierce as a hawk is Sokar, and terrible

is the punishment he metes out to those who re
against him. Hard by his dwelling is a l
where the water boils and bubbles with heat
water boils in a pot. Into the boiling lake
cast the rebels, and they cry to Ra for help,
Ra lies cold and lifeless, waiting for the com
of Khepera, and their cries are unheeded w
the Boat passes on its way.

On the farther wall of the ravine is a high i
vaulted building, the home of Night and Da
ness. Two birds cling on either side, and ro
about it glides a two-headed serpent. He l
his savage heads, and his poison is ever read
strike the rash intruder who should dare to
to pass. Faithful is his watch, for in the h
of Night and Darkness lives Khepera, the g
Soul of the universe, he whose emblem is
beetle, the god of resurrection. In the forn
a scarab he watches the coming of Ra, and
flies upon the Boat and awaits there the t
when he shall bring Life back to the god.
now through the thick darkness along the
row passage falls a gleam of light; the Mor
Star stands by the gate to lead the Boat
wards; for in the darkest of the night i
promise of the coming day.

Slowly goes the Boat of Ra, passing thro
the Duat, through regions of thick darkness
terror and dismay, to the place where the abon
able Apep lies in wait for the coming of

Thus passes the fifth hour of the night, and the sixth hour is at hand.   Then the goddess of the fifth hour makes way for the goddess of the sixth hour, and she calls aloud the name of the Guardian of the gate.   Flung wide are the portals, and the Boat of Ra passes through.

" Abyss of waters " is the name of the sixth country of the Duat, and Osiris has dominion over it, Osiris, the great god, Lord of the city of Daddu, the living King, Creator of men, of cattle, and of the green things which grow upon the earth, Osiris, to whom all men bow in praise and adoration.

The river rises out of the sand again, and the Boat floats upon its waters, and those who are in it rejoice, for the hours of the night are passing away.   On the banks of the river are the great shapes of the gods, mysterious and wonderful ; nine sceptres of sovereignty stand there also, and a monstrous lion looms through the darkness, faintly seen in the light which comes from the Boat of Ra.   Three shrines stand beside the river, and a serpent whose breath is flame guards each one.   Mystic and strange are the forms within the shrines, and to man it is not given to know the meaning of them ; in one is a human head, in another the wing of a bird, in the third the hind part of a lion.   Here also lives the great coiled serpent with five heads, and within his coils lies Khepera, god of resurrection.   On his

head he places the scarab, beneath his fee
the sign of flesh ; thus does he send Life into
dead, and thus will he re-vivify Ra. For th
the farthest point of the Duat, and beyond
gate lies the way to the sunrise.

Slowly goes the Boat of Ra, passing thro
the Duat, through regions of thick darknes:
horror and dismay, where the abominable A
lies in wait for the coming of Ra. Thus pa
the sixth hour of the night, and the seventh 1
is at hand. Then the goddess of the sixth :
makes way for the goddess of the seventh h
and she calls aloud the name of the Guardia
the gate. Flung wide are the portals, and the :
of Ra passes through.

"Secret cavern" is the name of the sev
country of the Duat. Full of danger and p
it, for the abominable Apep dwells in this
As a great and monstrous serpent does hera
and with wide-open mouth he swallows the w
of the river, that the Boat may be wr
and that Ra may perish. Then would the
belong to the powers of darkness, and evil
wickedness would overcome the gods.

But in the prow of the Boat stands Isi,
great enchantress, whose magic none can
stand ; Isis, the greatest of the goddesses, sh
can raise the dead, and to whom all mankin
love and reverence. With arms outstret
she recites the Words of Power ; calling

across the dark river.   Over the body of Ra, the
serpent Mehen casts his protecting coils, for now
is the time of danger.

On a sandbank in the midst of the river lies
the abominable Apep.   Four hundred and fifty
cubits long is the sandbank; the coils of Apep
cover it so that naught can be seen but the river
around him.   Loud does he hiss and roar, and
the Duat is filled with the thunder of his voice,
yet Isis flinches not, nor does she cease her
incantations and the magical movements of her
hands.   Her spells prevail and the abominable
Apep lies helpless on the sand.   Then Selk and
Her-desuf leap from the Boat of Ra and bind
him with cords, and with sharp knives they pierce
his flesh, hoping to destroy him.   But Apep is
immortal, and every night will he await and attack the Boat of Ra.   Yet Selk and Her-desuf
hold him fast while the Boat continues on its
way, past the great sandbanks, where he writhes
and twists and struggles to get free, but the cords
are strong and the knives are sharp and his efforts
are in vain.

Onward goes the Boat to the burial-places of
the gods.   These stand beside the river; high
mounds of sand are they, over each mound is a
building, and at each end the head of a man
watches the passing of Ra.

Softly goes the Boat of Ra, passing through
the Duat, moving through the darkness to the

7

sunrise and the day. Thus passes the sev
hour of the night, and the eighth hour is at h
Then the goddess of the seventh hour makes
for the goddess of the eighth hour, and she
aloud the name of the Guardian of the
Flung wide are the portals, and the Boat of
passes through.

"Sarcophagus of the gods " is the name o
eighth country of the Duat, for here dwell the
gods. Dead and buried are they, embal
and bandaged as men embalm and bandage
dead upon earth. They cry aloud saluta
to Ra as he passes, calling to him across the
expanse, but so far away are they that the s
of their voices is as the roaring of savage b
as the cry of birds of prey, as the wai
mourners, as the murmur of bees. Before
Boat go nine Followers of the Gods; stra
are their forms, mysterious and wonderful,
naught that is upon the earth. In front of t
march the four souls of Tatanen in the like
of rams, great and fierce, with horns wide-spr
ing and sharp-pointed. The first is crowned
high upstanding plumes, the second with
Red crown of the North Land, the third with
White crown of the South Land, the fourth
the glittering disk of the sun. Ancient is T
nen, dweller in Memphis, where the abode of l
is on the south of the wall.

Softly goes the Boat of Ra, passing thro

the Duat, moving through the darkness to the sunrise and the day. Thus passes the eighth hour of the night, and the ninth hour is at hand. Then the goddess of the eighth hour makes way for the goddess of the ninth hour, and she calls aloud the name of the Guardian of the gate. Flung wide are the portals, and the Boat of Ra passes through.

" Procession of images " is the name of the ninth country of the Duat. Full and strong runs the river, and the Boat is borne forward upon the rushing stream. Twelve star-gods guard the Boat, with paddles in their hands, ready to help the Boat in case of need. Thick darkness broods not upon this land, for twelve great hooded snakes lie coiled upon the bank, and the breath of their mouths is a flame of fire, gleaming upon the dark water and upon those who dwell in the Duat. Three shallops float upon the sombre river ; strange is the shape of these shallops, not like the boats of men ; and the shadowy forms within them are in the likeness of a cow, of a ram, and of the soul of a man. From them the dwellers in this land receive the offerings which are made to them upon the earth. Then the star-gods break into singing ; and the twelve goddesses and the weaving gods and the dwellers in this land chant the glory and honour of Ra, praising the Lord of the Boat, the Maker of earth and of heaven. With joy and singing they follow the appointed path.

Onward goes the Boat of Ra, passing through
Duat, travelling to the sunrise and the light of o
day. Thus passes the ninth hour of the ni,
and the tenth hour is at hand. Then the god,
of the ninth hour makes way for the goddes
the tenth hour, and she calls aloud the nam,
the Guardian of the gate. Flung wide are
portals, and the Boat of Ra passes through.

" Abyss of waters, lofty of banks " is the n;
of the tenth country of the Duat, and the r
is Ra. The dwellers in this land come to n
their king as he passes by upon the swelling ri
Deep and full and strong runs the stream,
the Boat is borne forward upon the rushing
rent. Divine warriors armed with glitte
weapons of war are a guard for their king; l
is on their faces like the light of the sun.
the side of the river are four goddesses; u
the darkness they cast beams of light, ma
bright the way of Ra upon the gloomy ri
Before the Boat of Ra moves the Star of M
ing in the form of a double-headed serpent w
ing upon legs, and upon his heads are the cro
of the South Land and the North Land; betv
his coils is the great hawk of the sky; Leade
Heaven is his name, for the stars of heaven fo
him, but men call him Hesper and Lucifer .
In a shallop on the stream is a snake, Life oÍ
Earth is he called, and he watches in the
against the enemies of Ra.

The greatest of all the countries of the Duat is this, for in this realm of wonder and mystery Khepera joins himself to Ra, and Ra himself is created anew. Yet the dead body of Ra remains in the Boat ; but his soul is united to the soul of Khepera.

Onward goes the Boat of Ra, passing through the Duat, travelling to the sunrise and the light of open day. Thus passes the tenth hour of the night and the eleventh hour is at hand. Then the goddess of the tenth hour makes way for the goddess of the eleventh hour, and she calls aloud the name of the Guardian of the gate. Flung wide are the portals, and the Boat of Ra passes through.

"Mouth of the cavern " is the name of the eleventh country of the Duat, and Ra is its ruler. Low has the river fallen and sluggishly it runs, and the Boat is drawn onwards by the gods ; not with cords do they tow it, but with the body of the great serpent Mehen, the protector of Ra. On the prow of the Boat is a fiery star, but its light is not redder than the strange and lurid glow which fills this land; terrible and red is it and the sight of it is full of horror. This is the region feared by evil-doers, for their punishment awaits them here. Far and near are pits of fire ; goddesses, whose breath is flame, guard the pits, holding in their hands gleaming swords of fire. With their knives do they torment the wicked and

cast them into the pits of flame till they p
utterly. Horus stands by and beholds
torments, for these are the enemies of Osiris
of Ra, doers of evil upon the earth and
phemers of the gods. No help can come to t
no escape is possible ; doomed are they by
own actions to the sword and fire. And
smoke and flame of their torment rise up in
Duat.

On the far side of the river are the st
Shedu is there in the fashion of a snake ; sc
and crimson is he, and the stars which for
body are ten in number. There also a sha
seen, mysterious and wonderful ; like a wu
snake with legs does he appear, and between
wings is the shadowy likeness of a man.
call him Atmu, dweller in Heliopolis ; anc
is Atmu, more ancient than Ra himself ; an(
sends the sweet breezes of the North Wind ι
the land of Egypt. On either side of him
Eyes of Horus show dimly in the faint and l
light. And now springs up the breeze of morn
gentle is it and slight, but with it comes
promise of the day.

Onward goes the Boat of Ra, passing thr(
the Duat, travelling to the sunrise and the]
of open day. Thus passes the eleventh hour,
the twelfth hour and the dawn are at h
Then the goddess of the eleventh hour m
way for the goddess of the twelfth hour, and

calls aloud the name of the Guardian of the gate.
Flung wide are the portals, and the Boat of Ra
passes through.

" Darkness has fallen, and births shine forth "
is the name of the twelfth country of the Duat.
On the prow of the Boat is the great scarab of
Khepera, ready to make the transformations of
Ra ere he reaches the end of the Duat. Not
like other lands is this twelfth region of the
Duat, for it is enclosed in the body of a vast and
monstrous serpent. " Life of the Gods " is his
name, and through this great and huge frame
travels the Boat of Millions of Years. Twelve
of the worshippers of Ra seize the towing-ropes
and drag the Boat onward, and here in the
body of the serpent is Ra transformed into
Khepera and is alive again, for now the journey
through the Duat is near the end. Standing by
the mouth of the serpent are twelve goddesses ;
to these the Worshippers of Ra yield the towing-
ropes, and they draw the Boat to the eastern
horizon of heaven. And now the dead corpse
of Ra is cast out of the Boat, as the husk is cast
away when the grain is winnowed out, for the
soul and the life of Ra are in the scarab of
Khepera, and the transformations of Ra are com-
pleted. With shouting and singing, with joy
and with gladness, the Boat of Ra passes out of
the Duat.

Glorious is the Manzet Boat, speeding to the

sunrise! Wide, swing wide the portals, and u
in the day. Between the sycomores of turqu
comes the Boat of Ra, and the mountain of Ba
is flushed with light. The serpent, guardian of
Great Green Waters, beholds Ra in glory in
eastern horizon of heaven, and the rays gli
on his scales.

Glorious is the Manzet Boat, borne upon
river, flashing in the splendour and the ligh
open day. In the foam at the prow of the B
sports the Abtu-fish, darting through the gle
ing spray, and the Ant-fish is seen in the whirl
of turquoise. From the earth rises up the so
of rejoicing, for all created things praise Ra at
rising.

Hail to thee, Ra, at thy rising; the night a
the darkness are past. At the dawn of the c
thou shinest, the heavens are filled with 1
light. King of the Gods art thou, all glory a
triumph are thine. The Gods come as dogs
thy feet, rejoicing to greet thee at dawn. H
to thee Ra, at thy rising; at thy coming all n
are glad. In joy dost thou come in the morni
with glory thou rulest the world. The stars
the heavens adore thee, the Gods of the ea
exalt thee, Lord of the Heavens art thou. H
to thee, Ra, at thy rising! None can expr
thy glory, Lord of all Wisdom and Truth. 1
souls of the East attend thee, the souls of 1
West are thy servants, the North and the Sou

adore thee. Worshipped art thou, our Ruler, by those whom thou hast created, Thou risest in heaven's horizon, thou causest mankind to rejoice. Hail to thee, Ra, at thy rising; at thy rising in beauty, O Ra.

NOTES

I. THE PRINCESS AND THE DEMON

Published : Prisse d'Avennes, *Monuments Egyptiens,* pl. xxiv.

Translated : Wiedemann, *Religion of the Ancient Egyptians,* p. 275.

This tale is sculptured on a sandstone tablet found by Champollion in the temple of Khonsu at Thebes, and now in the Bibliothèque Nationale at Paris.

There are twenty-eight horizontal lines of inscription, and above them is a scene of two boats of Khonsu borne on the shoulders of priests, with the king offering incense before them.

When first translated, the tale was supposed to be a record of fact, but now it is generally considered a folk-tale, redounding to the credit and glory of Khonsu, and therefore made use of by the priests of that god. The king mentioned in it cannot be identified with any of the historical monarchs of Egypt, although his personal name, Rameses, is sufficiently common among the rulers of the xxth dynasty.

II. THE KING'S DREAM

Published : Lepsius, *Denkmäler,* iii, 68.

Translated : Breasted, *Ancient Records,* ii, 810–815.

The inscription is sculptured on a round-topped stela of red granite, fourteen feet high, set up in the little temple which lies between the paws of the Great Sphinx.

The temple was excavated by Captain Caviglia in 1817. It forms the end of a processional way which leads downwards

107

by paved causeways and flights of steps from the edge o
desert into the sanctuary (see Vyse, *Pyramids of Gizel*
107). The tiny shrine is only ten feet long by five wide
at its farthest end, with its back to the breast of the Sp
stands this stela.

The inscription, which is in horizontal lines, is surmou
by a scene, duplicated to right and left, of the king m
a libation of water and burning incense before the figu
a Sphinx couchant upon a pylon or altar. The lower
of the stela is so mutilated that the inscription is eithe
stroyed or illegible.

The inscription purports to be of the time of Thothme.
a king of the xviiith dynasty, about 1400 B.C. ; erecte
that monarch as a votive offering. But from the evid
of the language in which the inscription is couched
obviously much later ; Erman dates it to a period betv
the xxiiird and xxvith dynasties. It may, however,
restoration of an earlier record, though of the early inscrip
nothing remains.

III. THE COMING OF THE GREAT QUEEN

Published : Naville, *Deir el Bahari*, ii, pls. xlvi–li ('
translation).

Translated : Breasted, *Ancient Records*, ii, 187–220.

The inscription, with the scenes illustrating it, are sculptu
on the walls of the temple of Deir el Bahari, on the n
side of the retaining wall of the upper platform.

The great building, known in modern times as the ten
of Deir el Bahari, was erected by Queen Hatshepsut of
xviiith dynasty, about 1500 B.C., for the double purpos
her own funerary cult, and of the worship of the god
Hathor. The chief events of the Queen's reign are sculptu
on the walls ; the record of her divine descent naturally h
a prominent place. The inscriptions in the temple v
wrecked and restored anciently, therefore much of the rec
is lost. Fortunately, however, Amenhotep III, a king of
same dynasty rather more than a century later than F
shepsut, adorned his temple of Luxor with similar scenes
inscriptions, relating to his own divine descent, changin

course the names of the mother and child and making a few immaterial alterations in the inscriptions. By means of this later example the whole of the earlier record is made clear.

The white colonnades of Hatshepsut's temple, set against a background of dark cliffs, form one of the most striking scenes in the valley of the Nile. The temple was used at one time as a Coptic village ; hence its modern name of Deir el Bahari, the Northern Convent.

It has recently been excavated and restored by Dr. Naville for the Egypt Exploration Fund.

IV. THE BOOK OF THOTH

Published : Spiegelberg, *Demotische Papyrus* (Cairo Catalogue).

Translated : Petrie, *Egyptian Tales*, ii, 89.

This story is written in demotic on a papyrus found at Thebes in the grave of a Coptic monk. It was among other papyri, written in hieratic and in Coptic, in a wooden chest, and is now in the Cairo Museum. Demotic is the script in which the latest form of the Egyptian language was written ; the earliest example remaining is of the reign of Shabaka of the xxvth dynasty, about 715 B.C. ; it continued in use till Roman times, when it was superseded by the Greek alphabet.

The papyrus is of the Ptolemaic period, but the exact date is uncertain, as the colophon at the end is partly illegible. The year 15 only is visible, which, however, is not sufficient guide to the reign of the king under whom it was written.

The legend given in this book is part only of a much longer tale ; it is in fact a story within a story, told by the *ka* of Ahura to the high priest of Memphis, when he ventured into the tomb of Nefer-ka-ptah in search of the Book of Thoth.

The Book of Thoth is said to contain only two pages; it must therefore have been a roll of papyrus written on both sides.

V. OSIRIS

Original : Plutarch, *De Iside et Osiride*.

Translated : Mead, *Thrice-greatest Hermes*, i, 278.

The treatise on Isis and Osiris was written by Plutarch, himself an initiate into the Osiris-mysteries, to a fellow-

initiate, a woman named Klea. It was written at
in the second century A.D.

It is the only connected account remaining of the de
Osiris and the wanderings of Isis. Though of so late a
it is found to be correct on the whole when checked b
inscriptions and sculpture of Pharaonic times.

The so-called Ritual of Denderah is our principal aut
for the worship of Osiris in the chief temples of Egypt
festivals of the month of Khoiakh. The Ritual is sculp
on the walls of the temple of Denderah, and gives in
detail the rites in use, and even the size and material
symbolical images. The inscription dates to the Ptol
period, but the Ritual is considerably earlier.

" Mystery-plays " of the death of Osiris and of the r
of Set by Horus appear to have been enacted on certain
occasions at the chief centres of worship. The pri
part was that of Horus, which was acted by the Ph
himself in the capital, and by the chief local notabilit
provincial centres.

VI. THE SCORPIONS OF ISIS

Published : Golénischeff, *Metternichstele* (with Ge
translation).
Translated : Budge, *Legends of the Gods*, p. 157.

This inscription is sculptured on a round-topped st
serpentine (?), fixed in a square pedestal. It was fou
Alexandria at the beginning of the nineteenth century
was presented to Prince Metternich by Mohamed Ali in

The front, back, and sides of both stela and pedest
sculptured with horizontal and vertical lines of inscri
and with mythological figures. The stela belongs to a
of amuletic objects, usually called Cippi of Horus, whic
inscribed with magical spells against all animals " biting
their mouths or stinging with their tails." This stela
largest Cippus of Horus known. On the front is sculp
in high relief the figure of Horus represented as a naked
standing on two crocodiles, and holding a lion, a g
scorpions, and snakes in his hands. He stands wit
shrine, which is surmounted by the head of Bes. Isi

Thoth, the goddesses of the South and North, and other
mythological figures and emblems are within and without
the shrine. Above this scene are horizontal registers filled
with figures, possibly representing scenes from legends which
are now lost.

The text which preserves the story of the scorpions of
Isis is inscribed on the back of the tablet, ll. 48–70. The
date of the stela is about 370 B.C., in the reign of Nectanebo I.
of the xxxth dynasty.

VII. THE BLACK PIG

Published : Naville, *Das Aegyptische Todtenbuch*, pl.
cxxiv.
Translated : Budge, *Book of the Dead*, ch. cxii.

The so-called Book of the Dead is a compilation of texts
which are found, written on papyri or on coffins, in the tombs.
No copy containing all the chapters is known ; the order has
therefore been arranged from a comparison of many examples.

The ancient name of these texts is " Chapters of Coming
forth to the Day " ; the modern name is " Book of the Dead,"
as it is evidently a manual for the use of the dead. It consists of a series of prayers, hymns, magical formulae, and
allusions to mythological stories, a knowledge of which was
considered necessary in order to escape the perils and dangers
of the life hereafter. It is obviously very ancient, for even
in the earliest known examples, the Pyramid Texts of the
vith dynasty, the text is often very corrupt. The Pyramid
Texts show traces of very primitive usages and cults, many
of which are lost in the later forms of the Book of the Dead.

The story related under the name of the Black Pig refers
to an incident in the war between Horus and Set, and is not
known elsewhere. Probably many such legends were current
in ancient Egypt, but few have been preserved to us intact.
Horus was the great hero-god, and, like the heroes of other
countries, he absorbed all the legends of local champions.
Some of his exploits and adventures seem to have been so
well known that a mere allusion was sufficient to recall them
to the mind of the reader. Sometimes a short and, to us

confused account is given, as in chapter cxiii of the B
the Dead, where the restoration to Horus of his han
arms, which have been lost in a swamp, is related in a r
which conveys very little to the modern reader.

A great number of legends have been preserved in n
papyri, but even among these the quantity of tant
allusions is larger than the number of complete le
Thus, in the Demotic Papyrus of London and Leyden, a
against fever begins " Horus was going up a hill at n
in the verdure season, mounted on a white horse." H
the gods eating, and they invite him to join them, l
refuses as he has fever. This is all that is said, bu
evidently an allusion to a well-known story.

VIII. THE BATTLES OF HORUS

Published : Naville, *Mythe d'Horus* (with French
lation).
Translated: Wiedemann, *Religion of the Ancient Egy*
p. 69.

The account of the war between Horus and Set is scul
on the inner part of the west side of the girdle-wall
temple of Edfu. The whole temple is dedicated to
though undoubtedly an early foundation, the present
ture dates only to the Ptolemaic period. It was beg
Ptolemy III Euergetes I, and took 180 years to bui
decorate. The girdle-wall, on which these scenes and i
tions were sculptured, was built and decorated about 10
either by Soter II or Alexander I.

The temple was excavated by Mariette, and is th
perfect in condition of all the temples in Egypt, fo
the exception of the wanton mutilation of the faces,
ably by Christian fanatics, both building and sculptu
untouched save by time.

The inscription appears to give in legendary form a
accurate account of tribal battles of a very early
Though the actual inscription is of a late date, many pri
ideas are preserved, especially in the hymns of the won
Horus. " Eat ye the flesh of the vanquished, drink
blood," is not a sentiment of the civilisation of Pto

times. Human sacrifice, however, appears to have been practised in Egypt at all periods. Harvest victims were burnt at Eleithyapolis (El Kab). Amasis II of the xxvith dynasty put an end to human sacrifice at Heliopolis; Diodorus says that red-haired men were offered up at the sepulchre of Osiris; as the king was the incarnate Osiris, this would mean that human sacrifices were made at the royal graves, probably during the funeral ceremonies. The Book of the Dead also continually alludes to human sacrifice. At Edfu an altar was found sculptured with representations of offerings in which human beings are the victims. Small figures, carved in the round, are known, which are in the form of bound captives; and show probably the method of binding the victim; the legs are bent at the knees, and the feet bound to the thighs; the arms are bent at the elbows and securely lashed to the body. This is not the ordinary way of binding a prisoner, but is a special method reserved probably for a human victim. The figures represent sometimes men, sometimes women.

Judging by the representations and scenes on the girdle-wall, a "mystery-play" was acted in the temple of Edfu, the Pharaoh playing the principal part, that of Horus. In early times it seems more than probable that Set, or the Ally of Set, was played by a human being, who was actually killed during the performance. When the custom of human sacrifice begins to die out, the human victim is often replaced by an animal. This is the case at Edfu, where Set is called a hippopotamus and represented as a pig.

IX. THE BEER OF HELIOPOLIS

Published: Léfébure, *Tombeau de Sety I*, pt. iii, pls. 15–18 (*Annales du Musée Guimet*, ix).

Translated: Wiedemann, *Religion of the Ancient Egyptians*, p. 62. (For a description of the tomb of Sety I see the Notes on Legend xi).

This story is sculptured on the walls of a side-chamber off one of the inner halls of the tomb of Sety I (room xii of the guide-books). On one of the walls is a representation of a cow standing under the star-sprinkled vault of heaven

8

This is Nut, the sky-goddess ; she is raised on the
hands of the god Shu, and each leg is supported by t
planets, and Boats of the Sun travel across her boc
connection between this representation and the l
quite uncertain.

The tale occurs only in this one place, but every e
hopes that he may one day find a tomb with a compl
of the story sculptured on the walls.

X. THE NAME OF RA

Published : Pleyte and Rossi, *Papyrus de Tu*
31, 77, 131–138.
Translated: Wiedemann, *Religion of the Ancient E*
p. 54.

This tale is found in a hieratic papyrus of the xxth
(about 1200–1100 B.C.). It is written on both sid
handwriting on one side differs from the handwritin
other, showing that it is the work of two scribes. The
is in black ink with occasional sentences in red. Hi
the running hand, derived from the hieroglyphs ; the
example occurs in the first dynasty ; it was supers
demotic in the latest period of Egyptian history.

This papyrus is not quite complete, but the part co
the legend is fortunately uninjured. The text con
magical formulae against the bites of serpents. In
by magic, the magician recited an event in the career
deity in which the god suffered from the same malad
human patient then seeking relief. The words whic
the divine patient would also cure the human invali
same idea prevails in the legend of the Scorpions of I

XI. THE REGIONS OF NIGHT AND THICK
NESS

Published : Léfébure, *Tombeau de Seti I.* (*An*
Musée Guimet, ix).
Translated : Jéquier, *Livre de ce qu'il y a dans l*
Budge, *Egyptian Heaven and Hell.*

The description of the Journey of Ra through th
World is sculptured on the walls of the tomb of S

NOTES 115

Thebes. This is the great tomb discovered by Belzoni in October 1817. The length is 330 feet, and it consists of long corridors,ⁱ pillared halls, and side-chambers, hewn out of the solid rock. The Book of Am Duat is sculptured on the walls of corridor iii, halls v, vi, and x, and side-chambers xi and xiii. Eleven hours only are given ; the twelfth hour, though frequently found on papyri, is rare in sculpture.

There are two versions of the Sun's journey through the Duat. One was called by the Egyptians themselves the Book of that which is in the Other World (Am Duat) ; the other has no Egyptian name, but is now called the Book of Gates, for in it the gates are more important than the countries which they divide. (For a comparison of the two books, see Budge, *Egyptian Heaven and Hell*). The Book of Gates is rarer than the Book of Am Duat, and is found sculptured on sarcophagi ; the finest example being the alabaster sarcophagus of Seti I, now in the Soane Museum in London.

The Book of Am Duat is found both in papyri and on tomb-walls, the earliest example of the latter being the tomb of Amenhotep II of the xviiith dynasty. It is a compilation by the theologians of that period ; an attempt to combine into one homogeneous whole several distinct ideas of the next world and the life hereafter. The fourth and fifth countries of the Duat are obviously one complete kingdom, ruled by the god Sokar, the Memphite god of the dead. As Memphis was a very important religious centre, its god of the dead and his kingdom had to be included in the Duat of Ra, in spite of the fact that it was a waterless desert, and that it ended with the Morning Star. It was a region totally different from any other kingdom of the hereafter ; no river ran through it ; it was inhabited by neither gods nor spirits, but by enormous and horrible reptiles. The ingenuity of the compilers of this Book in turning the Boat of Ra into a serpent, which could dispense with the river and glide over the sand, is certainly remarkable.

Another Morning Star appears also in the tenth hour, and the breeze of morning seems to be felt by the goddesses in the eleventh hour, for they raise their hands to shelter their faces from it. Budge (*Egyptian Heaven and Hell*) suggests also that the Egyptians looked upon the red clouds of the dawn as being tinged with the reflection from the pits of flame.

These indications of morning appearing in the wron,
point clearly to the fact of the book being a comp
more or less clumsy.

The first hour seems to have been added in order t
a good introduction to the compilation. The last .
evidently a compromise. The most ancient idea with
to the sunrise was that the Sun was born anew every n
of the Sky-goddess Nut. This theory does not fit w
dogma of the Sun's nightly journey through the
World in a Boat; therefore the last hour is represer
a dark and tortuous passage symbolising the womb
goddess. The birth of the Sun was the most importan
of the day to his worshippers, consequently the acce
the last hour is found frequently on papyri, buried
graves.

The Duat, or Other World, was generally suppose(
the region lying to the north of Egypt; the delta
Egyptians of the South; the Mediterranean and its
by the delta-people.

The Egyptians had an abridgment or summary
long account of Ra's night-journey. It was always
on papyrus in vertical columns, with all the scenes a
speeches omitted. It gives the name of each gate an
try and of the goddess of every hour; sometimes, tho
always, the names of the gods who live in the different r
and always the magical words of Ra to the inhabit
each land. Felicitous results here and hereafter are p
to all who know the words and scenes thoroughly.

The hymn to Ra is a paraphrase of hymns which
extant.

INDEX OF NAMES OF GODS

Abtu-fish.—A mythological fish which accompanies the Boat of Ra at sunrise.

Amemt.—The mythical animal which devours the hearts of the wicked at the Judgment of Osiris.

Amon.—God of Thebes. In and after the xviiith dynasty he became the supreme deity of Egypt under the name of Amon-Ra.

Ant-fish.—A mythological fish which accompanies the Boat of Ra at sunrise.

Anubis.—A jackal-headed deity who presided over the embalming of the dead. He was said to be the illegitimate son of Osiris and Nephthys, and, in the form of a dog, to have protected Isis in her wanderings.

Apep.—The enemy of Ra in the Duat.

Astarte.—A Syrian goddess, whose name is found occasionally in Egyptian inscriptions.

Atmu.—An early name of the solar deity worshipped at Heliopolis. In later times, the name of the setting sun.

Bes.—A bandy-legged dwarf with horns. God of music and pleasure, and protector of children. Possibly also a god of birth.

Besa.—A spirit of the corn.

Geb.—The earth-god, father of Osiris.

Harmakhis.—Horus on the Horizon, i.e. the sun at its rising and setting.

Harpocrates.—Horus the Child, son of Isis and Osiris.

Hathor.—Goddess of love and beauty ; often identified with all the other goddesses, including Sekhmet.

Hekt.—The frog-headed goddess of birth.

Her-desuf.—A form of Horus.

Horakhti.—The Horizon-Horus. The same as Harmakhis.

Horus.—The hawk-headed god is, properly speaking, the

117

brother of Isis and Osiris ; but is constantly confused with Horus the Child, and is called Avenger or Protector of his Father.

Isis.—The greatest of Egyptian goddesses, wife of Osiris, and mother of Harpocrates.

Khepera.—The rising sun, god of resurrection.

Khnum.—The ram-headed god of the cataract, who creates man upon the potter's wheel.

Khonsu.—The moon-god at Thebes.

Mehen.—The serpent who protects Ra in the Duat.

Mentu.—God of war.

Meskhent.—Goddess of birth.

Min.—Father of gods and men. God of Koptos.

Neith.—Goddess of Saïs. Identified by the Greeks with Athena.

Nekhbet.—The vulture-goddess of Upper Egypt.

Nephthys.—Sister of Isis and Osiris.

Nepra.—A spirit of the corn.

Nun.—God of the primaeval waters.

Nut.—The sky-goddess, mother of Osiris.

Osiris.—One of the chief gods of Egypt. Murdered and torn to pieces by his brother Set, re-vivified by Isis and Horus.

Ra.—The Sun-god, one of the chief gods of Egypt. Heliopolis (the On of the Bible) was the principal centre of his worship.

Sekhmet.—The lioness-headed goddess of Memphis.

Selk.—The scorpion-goddess.

Set.—Brother and murderer of Osiris. Looked upon, in late times, as the Author of Evil.

Shu.—Twin-brother of Tefnut. He holds up the sky above the earth.

Sokar.—The hawk-headed god of the dead. When fused with Ptah (Ptah-Sokar) he appears in the form of a mis-shapen dwarf, and is then looked upon as a god of resurrection.

Tatanen.—An obscure god, generally fused with Ptah of Memphis as Ptah-Tatanen.

Ta-urt.—The hippopotamus goddess of birth.

Tefnut.—Lioness-headed. Twin-sister of Shu. The two form the constellation Gemini.

Tepu-yn.—A spirit of the corn.

Thoth.—The ibis-headed god of all learning and magic. Chief centre of worship Khemennu or Hermopolis, now called Eshmunen.

Uazet.—Goddess of Lower Egypt.

Up-uaut.—The jackal-god of Siut.